Tapas of Tales

Life, love and adventures in Spain

Published by:

Palcho Publications

renate@renatevannijen.com

www.renatevannijen.com

Layout: Ferry Verhoeve

Table of contents

Preface

I was born on the 4th of April and you could argue that I was reborn twice after that. Firstly, when I went to Italy at twenty-eight, to study the Italian language for half a year. I stayed for one year and I was discovered as the artist that I've since been. Both by an art teacher and art enthusiast who told me "ma sei un artista!" (but you are an artist!) and by myself! I had considered myself to be a hobbyist till then, but this was the moment I was reborn and felt really happy and true to who I really am! My name in Italian, Renata, means reborn, how appropriate. I was invited to exhibit in the village of Gualdo Cattaneo in Italy a year later. So I went back to The Netherlands and I painted many paintings in the studio of a fellow professional artist. I learned a lot, had my first exhibition, sold almost all my paintings and left for Italy to stay for four more years. You can safely say that I'm actually a fan of Italy but life sometimes takes you on an unexpected journey. John was my partner at the time, an Englishman who I had met in England and subsequently lived with for three years in the Netherlands. We made the decision to try our luck in another country. That was not my first impulse to travel. I'd already experienced half a year on a Kibbutz in Israel when I was eighteen; a failed emigration to New Zealand at the age of twenty-one, which left me longing for the Netherlands after just one year, and then, of course, five fantastic years in Umbria, the green heart of Italy, had turned me into a world citizen. I didn't really feel at home in the Netherlands anymore. I wanted to leave again. John had an alcohol problem but was a so-called 'functioning alcoholic' and I hoped that this move would have a positive effect on his issues. He would rather we went to

Spain than to Italy and I thought "oh well, Spain is probably comparable to Italy". This is not the case in my opinion, but that is another book. John left three months before I did, to look for work as an English teacher. He had an impressive resumé and soon found a job in Logroño in the north of Spain. I followed in an old Citroën crammed full of my art and other stuff, and an aunt who kept me company during the trip. I soon found a part-time job as an English teacher at a language school, as making a living as an artist was too challenging at that time. Although John's alcohol issues were still a problem, the situation felt less intense than in the Netherlands. We lived and worked in Logroño for a year and then moved to southern Spain where I could work as a translator from Dutch to English and he as a proof-reader. After living together in Spain for three years, we broke up, but we remained friends and continued working together. No longer for a company, but as freelancers at home, for different customers. Our friendship lasted another six intense years in which he regularly knocked on my door because his alcohol addiction had turned his life upside down for the umpteenth time and he had lost everything. He then slept on my couch. After John had been in my life for twelve years, over six months after I had finished my book about 'living with an alcohol addict', we broke up. I wrote the book ('Cheers, Breaking the Silence ... One voice at a time') in English and he proofread it, which made him stop drinking for the next six months, but it didn't last. He went back to England and we lost contact. Writing helped me get things off my chest and was something that calmed me down. What remains now is the memory of the fun moments with this special man, very intelligent, with fantastic humour, but impossible to live with. We laughed a lot, even roared with laughter, and I will forever cherish these moments. However, my life went on and so did my Spanish adventure. I ended up marrying Miguel, a Spanish avocado farmer at the ripe old age of fifty-five. I was reborn again, this time as a married woman, something I had never dreamed of, wished for or even contemplated. Never say never as, as you never know where life takes you. In this book I share my special and funny experiences in Spain from the moment John and I arrived, the time we were separated, but remained friends, and my life with Miguel until now.

Renate

Pets in Spain

"We should have bought a few mountain bikes to get fit" is the overwhelming thought that fills my head when I run up and down the marble stairs in our home in southern Spain to separate our dog and cat. "Our family" had recently expanded with a new family member. We had thought about it for a while and had decided to save a less fortunate four-legged friend from an animal rescue centre. But it turned out differently. A few days later, when I went to our landlord to pay the rent for that month, I saw him. A fluffy little panda look-alike. He was about two months old and we fell in love with him. His story was sad enough. Dumped, somewhere on the side of the road by strangers, who clearly did not realise that the fluffy round ball with funny eyes was actually a poop and pee machine. John and I named him Chopra, after our favourite writer, because we thought there were plenty of 'Lucky's' in southern Spain. Chopra, soon became Choppy, and turned out to be a funny little chap with sharp teeth and much more energy than us. Deepak Chopra is a very calm person, but Choppy ... well the name says it all. He soon grew up into a short-haired border collie 'look-alike' with some Dalmatian traits. In the evening, when he was resting on the sofa, his blinking white eyelashes always endeared us. Especially after the daily struggle of disobedience, jumping and play biting. Not to forget, his grass, wood, toilet rolls and insect-eating, naughty behaviour. John and I went to puppy training every Saturday morning, conducted by a Danish neighbour. This was very necessary, mainly to train me to be patient. Then a nice English lady was looking for a home for her eighteen-month-old blue-eyed cat and we decided to take him in. Bluey and Choppy were first introduced to each other during two separate visits that showed us their mutual curiosity, without any aggression. A few weeks later, Bluey became part of the family. For two weeks we kept our doors and windows closed, to help him understand that the house with the overly enthusiastic playmate was now his home. Since then the evenings are no longer the same while Choppy is chewing on toys, our arms and Bluey's head. The latter is remarkably tolerant. We do our best to separate them when things seem a bit too rough. We have long been in love with these two creatures, and when I notice that I am irritated by another mischievous incident, I remember the wise words my mother would have said! "You wanted a bike ... now just pedal!"

Flashback

"No, ma'am, we cannot do that," said the man behind the counter of the Patrimonium housing association in The Netherlands. "Then you shouldn't leave." I had already saved ten years' worth of points in the rental housing system. All this time I lived in a tiny apartment in the centre of my hometown, Arnhem. I wasn't much of a city person and actually didn't feel very Dutch. I was born and raised in The Netherlands, but after leaving my homeland several times to try my luck abroad, my feet began to itch again. This time the decision was not that easy. I had passed the magic number of forty and then you start to think about the important decisions in life. Moreover, I was not alone this time. Four years later, there I was, building a new life in southern Spain. It seemed madness at the time in the Netherlands to decide to give up my protected life for an uncertain future. A very strong urge inside told me to go for it. Three years later. "It is sunny again," I realise whilst diving into the pool of our rental house. There is a strong wind. Something you can count on; every day around noon until about seven in the evening we are pampered by a cooling sea breeze. Today the strong wind blows pink and red petals in the water and it seems almost romantic, while the laundry tries to escape from the clothesline. From our garden we can also see a Buddhist centre, peacefully situated in the mountains. That reminds me every day of my desire to meditate, but the noise in my head is usually too loud. Meditating and communicating are a little similar, or perhaps I should say can overlap, in my experience. I like to communicate and there are so many pleasant ways to do this. Writing, cooking, painting, sculpting, all meditative activities that communicate something. But I also like translating, or just chatting away in a willing ear. My life seems to be about communication. After my daily swim, a shower and a large cup of English tea, I sit down at the computer to articulate the noise in my head. Thinking about my special situation today. It doesn't matter what problems I experience in building a new life in this special country. When it gets too much, I simply look around and relax. Conscious of the beautiful surroundings, the nice smile of an old Spanish lady, the sun, never far away, and the healthy air that I breathe. I think about what is happening in the rest of the world and cannot help but appreciate what I have. This is what I tell myself in those moments when the noise tends to become overpowering. Everything back in perspective. It was a good decision.

From euthanasia to butterfly

"I really like that about you" said my friend, "you can be so profound but at the same time you can deal with things in life in a really light-hearted way". The reason for my friend describing me this way was my reaction to a spoken message she left on WhatsApp about seeing the urn of a loved-one when visiting relatives. "It was so big!" she said and somewhat apologetic, she wondered whether it would bother me that she would talk about something like that. A reminiscent smile flickered across my face when I spoke into my phone, my finger holding the speech button in WhatsApp. "My father and mother used to go for a walk in a beautiful forest and moor area near our home town. When my mother 'prepared' herself to die she expressed the wish to have her ashes scattered on the moor. ALS, a progressive, neurodegenerative disease, had turned her body into a prison and after careful consideration by various medical doctors, and bearing in mind her very short life expectancy, she was allowed euthanasia. We held her when she peacefully went to the other side. Months later my father told me he had been to the moor to find the right place for her ashes. A white butterfly, totally out of season, kept him company, he explained. "'She' was fluttering from tree branch to shrub on the side of the path; staying in front of me close to me." Then my dad came to a crossing; it was the exact spot where my parents always stopped to decide to take a longer or a shorter route back to the car. The butterfly landed on a heath bush and did not move again. My father took it as a sign. A week later, on a beautiful sunny day in October, we walked the same route both my parents had walked so many times. My dad was carrying a very large cardboard cylinder with my mother's ashes. We stopped at the crossing. Just when my father opened the cylinder and started shaking it to liberate her ashes a strong breeze came up. He was covered from head to toe with her ashes and although I was standing a couple of metres away, my shoes were covered as well. For a split-second we were in shock to then burst out into laughter. It was so funny and through our tears of laughter and farewell we both felt it was my mother who had made it happen. I was sure she was laughing too and saying... "cheer up, I escaped my prison, I am happy!" To this day, almost 20 years later, I am reminded of that special moment, probably on a weekly basis, as white butterflies can be seen throughout the year on the Costa Tropical where I live. It is always a nice feeling, triggering a memory or simply 'love' when I say "hello mum" to the butterfly with a smile on my face. I believe there is more after death, but whether that is true or not doesn't really matter. What does matter is that you can sooth or even change certain feelings, and this can lead to changing situations, through the power of thought and imagination, through visualisation. This has been scientifically proven. Imagining that the butterfly is a sign from my mother changes my state of mind, it makes me smile, calm and happy. So, my dear friend, never apologize for a spontaneous reaction based on real life" I continued my message. I concluded with a smiley face, sending kisses and a butterfly.

On a drip

One moment I was napping in front of the TV and an hour or so later I was sitting with a drip in my hand. Well, you have to experience everything once, they say, and I had not experienced this yet. Also never thought that this could happen. Luckily, I had just painted my toenails a happy colour that morning and given myself a little pedicure. I had found a nice TV show to watch when Choppy wanted to go outside. I put on my flip-flops and went into the kitchen, where I put Choppy on his lead and opened the door to a small hallway leading into the garden. Suddenly I felt an incredibly intense, stabbing pain in one of my toes. Immediately I was unable to walk properly and began limping. I took Choppy out for a quick pee. Back inside the pain became almost unbearable and moved up into my foot. I was clearly bitten by something. I saw a very tiny drop of blood next to my toenail. I wondered what it was because I had not seen anything. My foot started to swell up. I put some ice on it, but that really hurt. I decided to grab a magnifying glass to take a better look. That's when I saw two tiny blood drops between my toes. "I've been bitten by a snake" I thought! I wasn't sure whether there were poisonous snakes in the area, but I decided to call the emergency services. They told me to come right away. I woke up my partner, who had passed out on the couch drunk a few hours earlier. My foot was hurting a lot and was very swollen, so I could not drive. I think the scary sight of my foot sobered up my partner, but I was praying all the way down to the hospital. It was totally against my principle to get into the car with someone who had been drinking. I have to admit that he drove very concentrated and calm and we arrived safely at the hospital "without wrapping ourselves around a lamp post" as he used to say. Once there, a doctor came to see me and told me it was good that I had come. He told me that they would take some blood samples and then, depending on the result, give me my medication, but that I had to wait for my turn in the first-aid waiting room. It was a fairly quiet evening. An hour later I was seen by the doctor. My blood was taken and I was given two tetanus injections. My blood pressure and temperature were measured and then I was sent to another room, to wait for the final blood results. I was given a drip. I was very surprised. I thought the doctor would say "oh, you have been bitten by a snake. Here you have an antidote injection and you can go home again." But I had to stay the entire night for observation. At half-past six in the morning my blood was taken for a second time and at eight o'clock I was seen by the doctor again for the final result. What I already suspected, because I wasn't drooling and shaking in the chair, it turned out to be a 'good-natured' snake that apparently is poisonous, but its poison is not dangerous for people. In the meantime, the swelling and the redness on my foot were almost gone and so was the pain. It only felt like a bruise when you pressed it. I had had three different infusions, one against the pain, one against the swelling and a large bag with liquid to clean my blood. My heart was also checked and they listened to my lungs. Quite an experience, being in a Spanish hospital waiting room. It was filled with mostly older people who were all put on a drip and were given an oxygen mask. It felt surreal. At eight o'clock I had my final consultation with the doctor who gave me ten large painkillers. I decided not to take them, since the pain was already gone. She told me that if my foot would start to swell or hurt again, or if I experienced something a weird sensation in my body (which I always do as I am a hypochondriac), I would have to come back to the hospital straight away. I was also given a week's worth of an anti-thrombosis medicine. Apparently snake bites can cause blood clotting. I had to inject myself, which wasn't a problem for me. I did take those injections as I would rather not become a 'thrombosis case'. On top of all this I received a prescription for antibiotics. I asked if that was really necessary and of course she said yes and explained that they were to prevent an infection. I decided to wait till the next day to see if the swelling would come back or if I would get a fever, as I really didn't want to take antibiotics. I was fine so I didn't take the antibiotics. I was surprised she didn't want to give me a cortisol injection and a few prednisone pills as well. If you ever need to go to a Spanish doctor these seem to be their preferred medicines to hand out. And if you have ever visited a pharmacy, you might have noticed that people often walk out with bags full of medicines. Scary really. But I can add another experience to my list and I learned my lesson ... no more walks in the dark in my flip flops.

A Spanish village

"Hiya", it sounds friendly, this morning greeting, by my Irish neighbour in the small white mountain village. "How are you?" "Fine thanks, and you?" I reply in passing without waiting for her answer, while my dog Choppy enthusiastically pulls me up the mountain for his daily needs. Walking up the steep streets several times a day for ten minutes and subsequently walking through beautiful nature for at least half an hour, guarantees me staying in a reasonable condition and keeping athletic calves. I walk through a vibrant world of Spanish aromas, roasted peppers and freshly baked bread and an abundance of fragrant jasmine and hanging geraniums that adorn the summer streets. Age-old small, and not-so-small houses rest lazily in the warm sun while the swallows loudly herald the summer. Almost at the top, some wizened old Spanish women and men, contrasting sharply with the sun-drenched white walls, wish me a 'buenos días'. With a smile, I wish them a 'good morning' as well. Every morning and evening they come together to chat on old plastic chairs. It is one of the few remaining Spanish scenes after the invasion of mainly English and Scandinavian foreigners who bought most of the village here for next-to-nothing some decades ago. I walk past the full parking lot at the top of the village, after which Chops can finally empty his bladder against a eucalyptus tree. Whilst he checks out various sniffing spots my heart starts beating faster when I walk the steep road up the mountain. At the top I take a little break. I have a fantastic view over Torrox that is peacefully beautiful when viewed from above, with a turquoise sea calmly glistening in the background. It's an enchanting image of this ancient Roman pueblo with traces of hundreds of years of Moorish civilization. A muddle of tiny streets with undulating walls often carved out of the rocks. The mostly blue sky embraces the silence in the streets, too narrow for cars in many places. All streets lead to the old square where the foreigners and tourists come together for a coffee, enjoying watching people passing by. I continue my walk. Sweaty but satisfied, we arrive at my age-old rental house an hour later. After a quick shower, I make myself a brown sandwich with the last bit of peanut butter and sit down to watch an episode of Frasier, which is possible because I have an English satellite dish. I decide to do my weekly shopping trip to various shops and supermarkets on the coast. It is a wonderful summer's day. My thin blouse is almost too warm. Nature spreads its abundance in a colourful display of poppies, wild lavender and wild daisies. I drive down the mountain and feel grateful for the breath-taking view of the Mediterranean Sea in front of me. Via the highway I reach the exit to Algarrobo Costa where I want to visit the Dutch supermarket, where I treat myself to a large jar of Dutch peanut butter, some salty raw herring, a bag of liquorice sweets and buttermilk. Back on the coastal road, which meanders through an almost continuum of coastal villages with inviting boulevards, I stop in Torrox Costa. There I buy some 'Deutsche Brötchen' at the German bakery and some sesame oil at the German organic store. I take a short break enjoying a delicious 'cappuccino' on the terrace of an Italian restaurant. Then I stop at the 'English shop' for some Quorn and English tea. Back home I hear my English and Irish neighbours yelling at each other ... with an excessive use of the F-word. Today I don't feel like working and as a freelancer I can organize my own time. Satisfied I install myself in front of the television with a homemade pizza for an episode of Morse. Another day of my life in Spain ... But that can feel very different sometimes!

Kissing in Spain

To kiss or not to kiss is not a very original title and I imagine that it has been used by many bloggers and writers alike, but it actually is a serious question when you have decided to pack up and move to another country. Or even when visiting friends or loved-ones who have undertaken the expat journey and who might introduce you to the locals. Being a European citizen is interesting in itself with all the different languages, but what might seem normal in one culture can be totally not done in a neighbouring country. Living in Spain comes with its own challenges and to kiss, how to kiss, or not to kiss is one of them. With such an array of nationalities flocking to the Spanish coasts you can easily be forgiven to get rather confused. I am Dutch and in Holland we do not kiss when we meet someone the first time. A friendly handshake and a smile are a more common way of greeting. However, when you get to the next level and become acquaintances, friends, or members of the same family, kissing the cheeks will be normal and three is the number of kisses exchanged. Having been living in Spain for many years I have become used to kissing total strangers when I am presented to someone. Two kisses are the norm. I usually end up doing the air kiss whilst receiving a wet or not so wet kiss on my cheeks. In a business situation the very first meeting might be a handshake, but when you walk out of the door, don't be surprised to get two kisses. This is what happened to me when I sealed the deal with a printer in Granada, who I had never met before and who is taking care of the print of my book, 'Reflections from La Herradura'. Luckily, he was a handsome fellow! I personally am not sure whether there is an 'official' side to start the kissing, but I usually start on the left. This can sometimes be a challenge - especially when presented to an old, more or less toothless goat shepherd - as there is always that fear that we do not start on the same side and end up planting a kiss full on the mouth, followed by awkward laughter and trying not to wipe your mouth too obviously. I also have a lot of friends and acquaintances from other nationalities, among others many British but also German, Italian, French and people from Scandinavian countries. The habits of kissing vary as some like to give four kisses, some just kiss once, but many people kiss twice, like the Spanish. It is even common for men in Spain - as it is in many Mediterranean countries - to kiss each other in public when they meet up. My late doggy, Choppy, also enthusiastically greeted everyone who entered with a kiss... A French one, quite slobbery. So, kissing in Spain can be an adventure and finding out specific rules and regulations seems to be a hard task. My advice: just go with the flow and see where it leads, or go for a hug! Yes, a hug, as this is something that seems to become more and more accepted and normal. A hug instead of a kiss when greeting someone you know! In many northern and southern European countries the hand-shake, with or without a kiss, might be preferred on first presentation, but once acquainted, a hug may be part of the greeting. Most of my friends and people I have met several times hug so I get my fair share of body contact. I never really think about the intimate character of pressing my body against the body of another male or female but it is usually a rather pleasant sensation. Curiously, the kiss is not necessarily used when you are hugging someone. But who cares, in this world of anger, hate, war and so many awful events it is simply nice to hold someone for a few seconds, allowing your heart to greet and connect with the heart of your fellow hugger. I realise once again that I am privileged to live in this beautiful, special country.

Wet knickers

"Hola, guapa!" It sounds a little hoarse to my ear. I'm in the local bakery in the square ordering a brown baguette … I look behind me to see the attractive Spanish bricklayer with distinguished grey hair greeting me with a smile. "*Igualmente,* I whisper back. My 'likewise' in reply to his flattering "hello, gorgeous!" gives his dark skin a red glow. It amuses me as this interaction is only happening in my head. For quite a few weeks now, our eyes have met every time I go to the square for a coffee, which is practically every day. He stands out from the other bricklayers because he seems to be the most skilful worker. The previously picture-postcard, idyllic square, with a beautiful Spanish fountain and benches made out of cement, covered with colourful Moorish tiles – was a perfect place to linger in the sun. It has changed into a modern square with misplaced grey, marble tiles, cold and unwelcoming. Nobody is happy with the new look, but the work goes on. I pay for my bread and walk towards a table in the square. I load up the free chair next to me with some daily shopping and order a 'café con leche'. I try not to make it look too obvious that I have picked a table with a good view of Pepe, as his colleagues call him. He must have sensed me sitting down as he looks up and our eyes meet, but we both furtively look away. Pepe decides which tiles need to be laid next. He is the one who puts them down with extreme precision, measuring everything carefully. It makes him look very attractive although I don't really understand why I feel little tingles in my belly. Sometimes he stands up straight to light a cigarette, but his breaks never last long, he is a hardworking man. In contrast, his colleagues clearly embrace the 'mañana' attitude. There is no haste in their actions; what will not happen today will happen tomorrow or the day after that. Every now and then, one of them cuts a tile noisily and passes it to Pepe, and then they all sit back from the effort, to watch Pepe put the tile into place disinterested expressions on their weathered faces. I cannot keep my eyes off Pepe, his slim muscle-toned body visible beneath his white T-shirt, his hands protected by white workman's gloves. Is this one of the last uncontrollable, subconscious urges of my body to start a family, I wonder? Feeling attracted to this very fit, hardworking man around my age... it is still possible, I'm still ovulating. I take a last sip of my coffee with warm milk and place the empty cup back in front of me on the white plastic table of the pavement café. I take out my notebook, which I use to write my daily experiences. *"It all feels rather exciting now that I know for sure that he realises I am regularly staring at him"*, I write, but my eyes drift away again, looking for Pepe. I don't see him and feel disappointed. Suddenly there is a tap on my shoulder. I am startled and look up. "Disculpa!" he excuses himself ... "can I offer you something to drink?" He doesn't wait for my answer but sits down self-assuredly. "I am Pepe" *he* says in a thick Andalusian accent. *"Hola Pepe, I am Renate... encantado!"* I say rather politely to make clear that his company is welcome. "Are you a writer? What are you writing about?" I tell him that I write about my life in Spain, but I feel embarrassed, afraid that he will understand that it is about him. He orders a red wine for me and a beer for himself. He has grey smiley eyes. I had not noticed that from a distance as my middle-aged eyes coupled with my vain habit to go through life without my glasses, turned my long-distance world into a blur. A pleasant blur, almost romantic. "*Salud*", I say when I hold up my 'vino tinto' and he his 'cerveza'. He neatly blows the smoke from his cigarette away from my face while we talk about the square, the tiles and his expertise. He is proud that I've noticed his skilfulness and offers me a generous smile, revealing his teeth. Quite a few are missing. It makes him look a lot older than he is, but I am already under his spell and he knows it. A little later we walk hand in hand to a small hotel in one of the back streets. I am terribly nervous and behave like a fifteen-year-old child. I giggle and stumble over a small threshold in the hallway, but Pepe catches me gallantly. I smell his musky skin and realise that our pheromones are mingling enthusiastically. Quickly we walk up the stairs to the small hotel room. It is clean and smells of wild lavender from the small vase on the side table. I have no eyes for that now though, only for Pepe. He takes off his shirt and it crosses my mind that he looks like a matchstick with his brown face and white body. I smile. The explosion of soft grey curls on his well-sculpted chest makes up for it. Passionately he pulls me against him. I feel as if I have ended up in the latest Mills and Boon novel. My breathing stops when he moves his hands, sensually, painfully slowly, but self-assuredly, downwards towards my hips. He kisses my neck and I feel my body reacting. I press it against his and listen to the accelerated beating of his heart. We kiss passionately while his hands explore the roundness of my body, delighted with my curves. He carefully pulls up my skirt and I feel his hands moving in the direction of my ... "*Hiya, can I join you? I fancy a 'tapa'!*" I am cruelly interrupted in my fantasy by my next-door-neighbour. From the corner of my eye I see Pepe, resting his body against a wall in a slightly tilted James Dean pose, secretly peeping at me while he lights another cigarette!

A few days later I am watching my wet knickers on the washing line as they flap in the full wind. I enjoy a few hours of early spring sunshine on my roof terrace with its view across to an enchanting rocky, sand-coloured mountain range interspersed with a dash of pine tree green. I notice the noise in my head. Too many thoughts, too many things I want to do but forever postpone. I think back to my life with my ex-partner, hearing his comments in my head. "Holy wet pants", he says with a big smile, because some of my briefs have holes in them. My mother also pops into my head, still worried about me in her afterlife. "Child, you should be ashamed of yourself, what will the neighbours think!" I don't really care what the neighbours think. I suspect that they find me rather strange! I often find myself strange and laugh about my own unusual behaviour, as I did this very morning. Still somewhat sleepily, I close the blue iron door of my small home that I rent in the Spanish white-washed mountain village. I walk up the steep narrow street with my dog Choppy, the white tip of his black tail enthusiastically waving in the fresh morning breeze. My favourite song, 'Aisha' sung by 'The Outlanders' enters my head via earphones. The slow-beat rhythm makes me want to dance; my step becomes lighter and a smile lights my face. Every now and then I feel the vibration of my voice singing along with a few words as we enter the green hilly area surrounding the village in the direction of the valley. It is still very quiet in the streets. Life never starts early in Spain, but a few cars full of bricklayers and bank employees are heading towards the village centre. I think about Pepe, as I do all the time. I feel a strong tingling sensation in my belly when I do and my mind drifts off into places I've never been before. Places of isolation where I can continue our get-together. Choppy and I walk through the valley which is lush with greenness after a long, wet winter. Almost an hour later we return to the village in the direction of the square. We pass through picturesque narrow streets and I notice my heartbeat getting faster. It is not because of my uphill walk, but I am painfully aware that I am getting increasingly nervous while approaching the square. I could easily have taken a different route to reach home, but I need to see Pepe, I need Pepe to see me, it is stronger than my common sense. Passing the square, I realise it is still too early for the bricklayers to have started their daily work so I walk back home, take a shower and walk out the door with my notebook and a shopping list. I always find an excuse to persuade myself to go to get something from one of the village shops surrounding the square. Legitimate excuses, I convince myself, but the truth is that I want to stare at Pepe. He is the one who makes my heart beat more rapidly, but I know that it starts to become a bit absurd that I cannot keep my eyes off him. When he looks back and our eyes meet, I rapidly look away, feeling caught and terribly shy. But today will be different. I need to create a change, I need to address this situation and say something to him, anything! Arriving at the square I must tread very carefully as the new tiles are extremely slippery and I don't want to fall flat on my face. I have to take small steps and straighten my back to maintain a good balance. In a stately manner I stride in the direction of the pharmacy. I pass Pepe and his colleagues who are working right in front of the highly-illuminated store. I am uncomfortably aware that my straight, somewhat unusual posture, makes my over-sized breasts stand out more than I would like, as a result of which I am not paying attention to the small entrance step. I stumble and cannot prevent myself from falling down in the most unflattering position. In a flash I realise that you should be careful what you wish for because it might come true, thinking back to my fantasy the day before. But it is not exactly the same. This time my stumble over a small step does not land me in the strong arms of Pepe. I feel extremely awkward, force a silly smile on my face and, too scared to look around me, I get up and quickly walk into the pharmacy to buy anti-varicose support panties. I feel so ashamed that I seriously consider staying in the pharmacy for the rest of the day but it is only ten o'clock in the morning, so I pull myself together and walk to the pavement cafe where I strategically sit myself down at a table with a good view to the entrance of the cafe where Pepe is now having his morning break with a coffee, a glass of brandy and a cigarette. Out of habit, and without asking me, the barman brings me my 'latte'. I like that. I realise that it will only be a couple of days for the square to be finished and Pepe to disappear from my life. I have to say something; I have to let him know my feelings. After his break he walks out of the cafe and I seize my chance. "Oiga", I say, to attract his attention ... "Do you have a minute? I just want to say something." Nervously and astonished he walks towards my table and, as if from a distance I hear myself say: "you must have noticed that I have been staring at you for weeks now . . . I want to apologize for that. I didn't want to make you feel uncomfortable!" I also wanted to tell him that I fancied him, but the words simply didn't come out of my mouth. "Sorry," I say once again. Pepe smiles and in English with a strange accent and far too loud he says "OK!" I know the spell has been broken. Sadly, I cast my mind back to the weeks full of desires, sexually-excited feelings, juvenile behaviour, secret thoughts and wonderful butterflies fluttering around in my belly. Pepe has walked back to the square now. Just before getting ready to bend down again to lay a few more tiles he adjusts the bulge in front of his trousers I quiver like a butterfly! Talking about wet underpants …

The fishing net

It was difficult to find one of those plastic, children's fishing nets with a long handle. I finally found one in a souvenir shop, mainly aimed at children's beach fun. The green fishing net, with a long handle, now looks a bit out of place in the corner of my bathroom in my home in the mountain village. It is 10 o'clock in the evening and from the window I look over the roofs of the whitewashed houses, with the mountains as an impressive backdrop, and here and there a sparse white villa. I have the feeling that I live in a different dimension, so far away from the Netherlands. Through the bedroom, adjacent to the bathroom, I walk to the balcony and take a seat on one of the two wicker chairs. The paint is peeling off, but they are still comfortable. A late-evening sun creates an impressive golden spectacle on the mountain range. Fascinated, I absorb the environment. It never gets boring. Time passes and suddenly I realise that the night has fallen. It is still warm. Bluey comes and sits next to me on the edge of the balcony. It always looks somewhat dangerous and messy as he manoeuvres his big bum in a, for him, comfortable position, balancing like a rope dancer. Like a king he oversees his empire where he will, undoubtedly, undertake his nightly voyage of discovery on the rooftops and roof terraces of the neighbours. Satisfied, I get up and walk downstairs to make myself a cup of tea. I sit down on the sofa, take the controls and switch on the television. My favourite show starts in a few minutes. Suddenly I hear a strange noise. My heart starts beating nervously quickly. "What is happening? Is there someone upstairs?" I gather all my courage and walk back up with a rolling pin in my hand. Bluey sits on the floor of the bathroom and stares at the ceiling. His prey is trembling and clings with fear of death in the corner of the ceiling. I'm happy to be on time, just before the inevitable 'kill'. I grab the green fishing net and carefully place it over the shaking dark tiny body of the bat. With a broom, I cover over the net and walk over to the balcony. The bat flies towards its freedom and disappears into the dark night. Two weeks later. I hear some strange sounds, somewhat indefinable in the distance. I wake up from a deep sleep and vaguely realise that my bathroom is being transformed into a 'killing field'. But I am too tired to really realise what is going on and turn on my other side to immediately return to my dreamland! "Crunch, crunch" I am sucked back into reality! It sounds different from the usual crunchy sound of my cat nibbling on its dry food in the bathroom. I feel irritated and get up. I switch on the light in the bathroom. Bluey is standing bend over the bottom part of the body and the long tail of a small field mouse, which probably got lost in the labyrinth of rooftops. Bluey looks up. His blue eyes stare into mine. I chase him away. Nauseous with the idea that he has just eaten the head and upper body of the mouse, I put the rest of the little body in a bag and throw it into the bin downstairs. I walk back to the balcony, in need of fresh air. The full moon creates a beautiful glow over the roofs of the white village houses. I stare at the starry sky and wish for a shooting star. I still have a few wishes that I would like to see fulfilled. Bluey jumps on the edge of the balcony balustrade. He smiles at me, I'm sure, but I'm tempted to give him a little push. I restrain myself, but I realise "today I really don't like cats".

A downward spiral

Everything seems to go wrong; I feel like I'm sucked into a downward spiral. My body, my faithful laptop, suddenly not so loyal anymore, and car problems seem to accumulate whilst the start of the crisis is having an impact on my translation work and selling my art during a time of crisis is even more challenging. I still have to postpone buying a new computer because of my financial situation. I remain cheerful and am surprised that I am not falling into a major depression. The weather has also left its marks. It has been an incredibly long, rainy winter, unusual for southern Spain. The Costa del Sol, a title that suddenly doesn't feel so apt anymore. Wet, cold, and especially humid. The walls of the village houses cannot cope with the unexpected heavy rainfall that has been going on for weeks. My white bathroom with blue tiles has changed into a black and white bathroom with blue tiles. Black mould covers the walls. And the toilet doesn't really cooperate either. The English plumber, called in by the landlord, doesn't understand his profession. He still hasn't sorted the problem after five visits. I suspect he used to be an office clerk who chose a life in the Spanish sun. The toilet situation is annoying, but I'll manage to live with it. Much more alarming seems to be the fact that almost no translation work comes in, and I have to suppress the panic that I feel when I realise that I don't know how to pay the rent next month. An accumulation of worries. The news that my car needs a large repair also doesn't help. My old, much beloved car. She had done so well for a long time; the dust-free spot on the dashboard a silent witness to the proverbial pat on the back that I regularly give my car. But she obviously is starting to give up on me. It sounds like she needs a new drive belt and the shock absorbers are shaking. The lights are not shining all that bright anymore either. When I use the direction indicators, the high beam turns on and the low beam only works occasionally. That the front and rear bumper are held together by radiator adhesive tape suddenly seems a trivial matter. Fortunately, I live in Spain where the rules are taken a little less seriously. The garage owner, who gave me the bad news of a minimum of seven-hundred-euro repair, advised me to first go to the annual, mandatory car inspection. I went that same week, so it seemed logical to get checked out whether there were other problems preventing my car from passing the inspection. A prayer in advance must have helped because even I, can recognise the many flaws. The gods were apparently in a good mood, and to my surprise the car was approved again for another year. Sadly, the repair costs are too high and the car is no longer worth it. As a result, I just keep on driving and hope that she will continue for a while, with all the stress of uncertainty that this entails. A large mug of hot strong tea with milk makes up for a lot. I manage to relax a bit and my mind wanders. "Surely, there will be a change in my uncertain situation" I wonder as I rub a sore spot on my leg. It feels hot and is red and slightly swollen. I don't think too much about it and suspect that it is an 'unhappy varicose vein'. I sit back and relax on my sofa and dial the number of my cousin with whom I have telephone contact every week. I tell her about my painful leg and ten minutes later, on her advice, I am in the waiting room of the 'Urgencia', for a consultation that is not covered by my insurance. It is news to me that the risk of thrombosis runs in our family, and suddenly I feel pains and a tight feeling on my chest and everywhere else. Stress no doubt. A syringe with blood thinner in my belly later, the unfriendly ancient doctor, because he looks as if he is ninety years old, adds my story to his computer. I pay the eighty euros for my treatment and walk back home with a bag full of medicines. The next day I go to the doctor's post in Nerja, covered by my insurance, which is a good thing. The young doctor prescribes a full blood test, a twenty-four-hour heart test with a Holter and an ultrasound of my leg. I suddenly feel very sick and pathetic. A little panicky too. Back home, I decide to try and forget the situation and to concentrate on something else. I grab my favourite notebook with a nice leather cover and think back to a few days earlier when I received a visit from Beate. I write 'Best friends' ...

Best friends

She would like us to become best friends. She is short, abundantly curvy and her grey, very short hair does not really flatter her white face. But the colourful blouse with a bird of paradise print turns her into a really pleasant appearance. She greets me with a bright smile at the Nerja Arts Festival, where I have an exhibition, and she says "Hi, I am Beate". She turns out to be a fan of my work and buys my entire series of mandala cards. Soon it becomes clear to me that she has all the time in the world and I listen to a waterfall of words. She gives meditative dancing classes in front of a German café on the 'costa' and asks if I want to join. I explain that it is not really my thing, but promise to meet up with her sometime soon for a cup of coffee. Three months later my phone rings. "Beate here." She explains that some of her friends from Germany would also like to purchase my mandala cards. Hopeful she asks whether they can come and visit me in my studio. I hesitate, because saying that I am a messy person is quite an understatement. I look around the small old house that I am renting in the middle of the typical white-washed Spanish village and realise it is littered with stuff. A dining table filled with two bowls of fruit, all sorts of bits and bobs, including my computer and keyboard and lots of papers and unopened bank statements. The state of almost every other surface in my house is not much better. Books on various bookshelves look cluttered with sheets of paper bulging out. Fluff balls of dog and cat hairs are scattered around the tiled floor as I have not vacuumed the house for over a week. My ceramic statues are collecting dust. The old white walls are filled with paintings and in every other room in the house there are paintings stacked against the wall due to lack of space. My studio in the small garden is disorganised with too many plastic boxes filled with painting materials and brushes and tubes of paint lie scattered on the large table. There are tools and empty plant pots everywhere on the floor. I take a deep breath whilst deciding that I'm not in the mood for a huge clean-up and suggest meeting up on the village square. Beate assures me that she and her friends don't mind a messy house, so we agree to meet near the church. I am introduced to three grey-haired, elderly ladies. They look very polite and tidy with their wrinkle-free, white blouses all buttoned up and no make-up on their slightly pink faces. Feeling a sense of panic as we walk towards my home, I apologize for the messy state of it, but they wave my worries away as they too are messy when on holiday they explain politely. However, there is no doubt in my mind that my mess is in any way similar to what they understand it to be and surely, they will be tempted to call in the Spanish equivalent of the public health service to help me declutter. I clench my teeth and together we walk to my house. One and a half hour later, more than 100 euros richer and some mandala cards poorer, I'm perfectly happy on my balcony. Swallows skim right past my head. The late evening sun envelops the mountain range in a fairy-tale orange glow. White houses in the valley glister like gold leaves in the distance. The sound of the swallows is reminding me that summer has arrived. And Beate and me? We are now best friends.

Spanish sounds

Thinking about Spanish sounds, flamenco music quickly comes to mind, and rightly so, but what about those other sounds? Like young men driving around in their cars beeping their horns to celebrate the winning of yet another football cup. Or the tail of cars, beeping their horns, following an expensive-looking vehicle dressed for the occasion with flowers and bows, transporting a wedding couple from the church to the party venue. Or the extremely loud bangs, which unfortunately create a lot of fear in most animals, used to mark the start and finish of a local festival of 'fiesta' on a daily basis, for as long as the festival lasts. Those typical Spanish festivals with live music starting at midnight on the local square, lasting till five or six o'clock in the morning. Most villages also hold an annual main village festival which usually includes a fair with lots of loud attractions, each trying to outshout each other with their own deafening 'disco' music to attract people. Those festivals usually end with a firework display with again an overdose of loud bangs and explosions. You could easily come to the conclusion that Spain is a very 'noisy' country and that the Spanish are very sound tolerant. But there is also the pleasant sound of the coffee-machines in the bars, grinding their coffee and heating up the milk for the next milky coffee. I am listening to it right now as I sit here in my favourite seafront café. I listen to the chit-chat that surrounds me in a mixture of languages from all over Europe, including Spanish of course. People often feel that Spanish people talk very loudly when they have a conversation and it always sounds as if they are arguing. I think this is not necessarily true. Yes, there are people who talk loudly but when you don't understand a language it can easily seem as if all the words are glued together, and that people are angry when they talk. However, there does seem to be a large number of people, both men and women who have a very raw, husky voice in Spain and I used to think that this was a case of too much tobacco over too many years. However, I changed my mind when, the other day, I heard a very young boy, somewhere between eight and ten years old, talking with that same husky voice. It actually makes me wonder whether the tone of our voice can be influenced by what we hear around us when growing up. A strong wind is picking up and I hear the soothing sounds of waves on the pebbled patches of the beach. It brings me back to my pleasant reality on a day like this in June. The month where spring turns into summer way before the twenty-first, a month of excellent temperatures, warm during the day and fresh during the evening and the month where the sounds become even louder. More people, more happiness, more live music and dancing and more noise in the apartments next door. It is all part of living here.

Summer

Seven o'clock. I turn off my cell phone alarm. An enthusiastic lick in my face tells me it's time to get up. With difficulty I drag myself out of bed and stagger to the bathroom. A loud scream of pain from Bluey, my cat, makes me jump ... and I am surprised that my weight has not crushed his little fluffy paw. Out of balance I stumble over the green fishing net that stands against the wall on the first floor of my old village house. It reminds me of the bat, which Bluey had dragged as booty into the bathroom. Since he has made the rooftops of the Spanish village unsafe, he has the summer habit of going hunting bats instead of the usual birds, salamanders and geckos. I am sure he has discovered their resting place somewhere under the eaves. I am happy with the fishing net with which I have been able to give freedom to many a rescued bat. Still a bit sleepy, I wash my face with cold water and brush my teeth. Choppy is wagging beside me impatiently, ready for his morning walk. I quickly put on my trousers, a summer blouse and my hiking shoes. Downstairs I just have time for a few sips of apple juice and there we go. A hysterically happy dog and me, much less happy, wondering why I wanted pets so much. A cool breeze accompanies me this summer morning. Dozens of swallows show their perfect flying behaviour while they sing their familiar song. I am overwhelmed by flashbacks from summer vacations in remote countries. Such a remote country where I now live. Suddenly I feel perfectly happy and a smile lights up my face. The cool morning breeze cannot prevent my firm morning walk from opening my pores. I realise that the summer has really started and I have to laugh at my somewhat strange appearance with my messy long hair, a bit wild and sticky around my face. I wonder what they think of me, a Dutch artist, withdrawn and living like a hermit, in a busy Spanish village, on my daily walk through the valley and the village with Choppy. An explosion of embarrassing drops of sweat are rolling out of every conceivable pore of my body and now soaked in sweat. I'm more or less creating a 'wet look', and I feel like I'm just displaying a little too much of my body. I see the eyes of the early peasants working their land with aubergines and courgettes, almost rolling out of their eye sockets, as they clear their throats, and greet me with a hoarse "Hola, buenos días". At the end of my morning walk, I decide to stop at one of the cafes on the square for a cup of coffee and a 'pitufo con tomate', a delicious typical Spanish toasted baguette-type bread, with tomato pulp and a little salt and olive oil. Regardless of my embarrassment, I pretend that my wet look is the latest fashion trend. The village has now also come to life and the first groups of ladies are chatting loudly at the table next to me whilst I enjoy the coffee and my breakfast. I observe. My favourite activity. Soon I cannot stop looking at the many bare feet in colourful, but uncomfortable-looking high-heel pumps and health sandals. An invasion of 'flip-flops', in bright cheerful colours with exotic designs, with or without a wobbling rubber flower. I am surprised at the shamelessness of some of the ladies who pass my table. With peeling nail varnish that barely conceals the unwashed state of their toenails that are too long, they nevertheless cheerfully flaunt their appearance to the world. Cracked, yellowed heels carry smooth legs free from unflattering hair growth. I'm fascinated by the ease with which some elegant ladies show their feet, deformed by the many years in which they have been squeezed into too small, pointed pumps with unhealthy high heels. The expensive leather of the brand sandals can hardly conceal the unsuccessful attempts of yet another expensive pedicure. Corns, dried-out and broken blisters and plasters with black edges scream for my attention. I seem to be surrounded by damaged, painful-looking unattractive feet. Nobody seems to care and I wonder why I do. I drink my coffee but leave my sandwich, suddenly not so hungry anymore. I pay for my drinks, get up and discreetly try to wipe away the puddle of sweat that my body left on the red plastic San Miguel seat outside the cafe. Finally, home again. Good dog, Chops! Now, for a cold shower!

True love

Unisex fashion is not so sexy says a voice in my head, but nobody cares about what I think whilst I'm enjoying a sparkling water with lemon on a terrace by the sea. I'm sure it's true love. They wear the same type of flip flops, the same colour bermuda shorts and the same T-shirt. I'm finding it a bit strange, but I also feel some jealousy coming up. Someone who loves you so much that he wants to wear the same colours. Hand in hand they stroll on the boulevard. The morning is still awaking. I look at the mainly German population who have come to the Spanish Costa to escape the cold German winter. Without any sense of shame, with their shirts waving in the wind, they happily expose their naked big bellies to whomsoever is watching. They all seem to wear blue camping slippers that you can buy in the local tourist shops for two Euros, often one size too small. Grey and bald elderly men and ladies with well-looked-after hair, firmly held together by a strong hair spray, dominate the street scene. All here for the sun and to enjoy life. An invasion of emigrants. Retired and non-retired dreamers who put into practice a long-cherished wish to live in the sun. Some come here with the wish to start their own business. Opening a bar or restaurant without any experience in a country where you don't speak the language, seems normal here. There isn't much integration. Former office clerks from other countries become construction workers, plumbers or gardeners and often only serve their own countrymen, disillusioned by the language barrier and the mañana culture. I actually don't have a problem with that. Clubs and groups are formed that regularly come together and I've joined an English writing club myself, which is really enjoyable. I look at the always beautiful sea. A pleasant wind massages my face and the soft rustling of the waves on the beach creates a pleasant calm in my head. I order a cafe con leche. It is getting busier on the boulevard. It is June and the first holiday makers are easy to recognize. From the skin you can guess who lives in Spain, with only a light, healthy complexion in the face and on the arms. If you can sit in the sun all year round, the urge to sunbathe will automatically decrease in my experience. Those escaping the northern winters often have a dark brown skin that is reminiscent of camel leather bags. They gave up fighting against a wrinkle-free face years ago. Holiday makers can be recognized by their bright-coloured summer clothing. The Germans are wearing neat bermudas and ironed shirts. The English can be recognized by shorts and lurid T-shirts that reveal the artwork of many talented and less-talented tattoo artists on milky-white, red or freshly tanned skin of their arms. There are almost no children, just a few miniature dogs that make being old a bit more bearable for many apartment-dwellers. The beach is now dotted with sun worshippers. I look at the seemingly lifeless bodies. Big bellies with stretched out arms and legs, lie larded and baking in the warm sun, cooled by a fresh sea breeze. Elderly women's breasts fall unflatteringly to the side of tanned bodies. It makes the idyllic picture a bit morbid. "They look like dead corpses that have been washed ashore," goes the thought through my mind. The elderly Spanish ladies and gentlemen who also stroll along the boulevard don't seem to mind this strange spectacle. They can be recognised by men dressed in grey trousers and a light-coloured shirt with short sleeves and the ladies by their usually short hair, tight sweaters with flowers or glitter and very neat skirts. "There is a large cultural contrast," I realise. It is time to go, I close my notepad and pay for the bill. I get up and see that an attractive man of my age is sitting down at the table next to me. He is wearing a white T-shirt and jeans, just like me. But his flip flops don't look like mine, what a shame, I wouldn't have mind a 'unisex' adventure!

Meditation

Priority lists lie scattered around every conceivable surface in my house. My head is overflowing with plans and things I have to do. I always make new lists because I can no longer find the old ones or have finished a number of points on the list but forgot to cross them out. I get tired of discussions, worries, postponing decisions, dreams about the future, fears about how things will go, and other thoughts that scream for attention in my head. The meditation CDs are just gathering dust in a draw. My bookshelf contains a large number of inspiring books full of good advice and tips, which I still want to read, but I always have better things to do. To try and escape from my over-active mind for a few minutes, I often lie down on the sofa, but that doesn't really make the 'noise' in my vivid brain any calmer. I know that I have to create space in my head and I long for a bit of mental peace. I decide to join a meditation club. Full of expectations, I open the fuchsia-coloured garage door draped with bright red hanging geraniums. I walk down the typical Spanish stairs, tiled with beautiful Arabic tiles, into the garden. I am warmly welcomed with an embrace by the Italian brother and sister who live with their mother in a stately home on the outskirts of the small seaside town. A colourful mix of interesting people of various nationalities trickles into the garden. Birkenstock sandals, Yves Saint Laurent pumps, elegant summer dresses, Indian hippie and casual clothing create a colourful decor. The Italian hostess serves a fragrant herbal tea in beautiful red Moroccan glasses. After the tea we all put our shoes on a shoe rack outside the door and enter the orange-coloured room to spend an hour together in silence. There is little light; some walls are covered with beautiful Indian rugs. There are candles on the floor in the middle of the large room and it smells of incense. Soft Tibetan sounds fill the room. Against the wall cushions are placed invitingly on the floor for us to sit down on. The host is sitting at the end of the room with a large gold-coloured gong. He explains what Zen meditation entails and how long it will take. I sit down with my back to the wall, in a cross-legged position, and I am painfully reminded that this once was very easy for me. It's a long time ago. I try to ignore my stiffness and close my eyes. I take a deep breath and concentrate on my breathing. Breathe in ... breathe out ... I follow my breath through my mouth into my lungs but soon I feel a tense sensation in my chest. I recognize this as a sign of stress, which often happens to me when I am in a somewhat uncomfortable situation. My head fills itself with the usual flow of information. I was told that I must leave these thoughts for what they are, look at them as from a distance, but it doesn't work. Five minutes into the meditation, my lower body starts to shake and tingle. It feels incredibly uncomfortable and a panic takes hold of me when I realise that I have to sit here for another forty-five minutes. Afraid to move, I can almost imagine that the jumble of words in my head can be perceived by others. I try to relax in my pain, which helps a bit. I have to sneeze and test the 'mind over matter' theory. To my surprise it works. I try to visualize the flow of words leaving my brain. I place them on clouds that I then blow away with a deep exhalation. But they immediately come back, like a black thunder cloud. My body is starting to hurt everywhere. I feel muscles and bones that I have never felt before and as if my head is about to explode. Aware of how my gut works, I have to fight against the natural tendency of my body to emit some air. I break out in a sweat and I have to tighten every sore muscle in my body. The fifty minutes of meditation seem like hours. Finally, the sound of the gong heralds the end of the meditation. I gently stretch my legs, which causes intense pain. We all pretend it's normal. Outside in the garden again, I finally fully relax and with a smile on my face I welcome the silence in my head. Next week I will definitely be back!

Finally home

When John and I arrived in southern Spain, back in 2004, we regularly explored the area. We discovered La Herradura and I immediately fell in love with the beautiful bay. It took almost ten years before I finally had the opportunity to move to La Herradura. It felt like coming home. There was a certain energy that appealed to me. A typical Spanish old fishing village with a special history. Not everyone feels at home in this village though. As the English say "you either love it or hate it". I found a nice, and at that time affordable, apartment with a big terrace where I could paint and write. Something that is important to me being an artist and a writer. I had split up with my then partner and was looking forward to a new life. La Herradura is still very Spanish. Many people from Madrid and Granada have a second home in the village and especially in July and August it is predominantly filled with Spanish tourists. Although there are quite a few foreigners attracted by this, in my eyes, magical village, it still feels really Spanish. When you visit a restaurant or a pavement cafe, you are almost always surrounded by a mix of Spaniards, including women from the village itself, and foreigners. Due to an influx of artists, writers, dancers, musicians, but also hippies, spiritual people and pensioners from all sorts of countries, such as Scandinavians, Americans, Italians, British, Irish, Dutch, Germans and much more, it has really become a cosmopolitan village. La Herradura fills me with inspiration to paint and to write my books. The word 'herradura' means horseshoe. The village embraces the bay shaped like a horseshoe. It is also very popular with divers, because apart from being one of the best diving spots in Europe, you can dive here all year round. Not that I do that. I leave it to others who like to hoist themselves into some unflattering and uncomfortably looking tight rubber. I would rather enjoy my walk along the sea with my dog and have a coffee with friends or enjoy a drink with a tapa somewhere. But what is clear, I feel at home here. I could write a book about it ... oh yes, I already did that, in English. It is called 'Reflections from La Herradura' and if you want to know more about this special village, I can recommend it. But for more funny adventures you can continue reading!

Welcome to Spain

So, you've made the move or are thinking about making the move. Or perhaps you just love coming on holiday to Spain. Maybe you've got yourself a small Spanish-English language book from your nearest bookshop and try to memorize and pronounce a few sentences correctly, even though you probably know that being able to ask for something in Spanish is pretty much useless if you won't understand the answer. Perhaps you did go to Spanish classes and can order your food and drinks and buy in local shops. Maybe you didn't because you were planning to go to an expat-dominated area of Spain, with a perfectly well functioning 'sub-society' if I may call it that, where you can offer your services to people who speak your language, in the Spanish sun. It can create some rather funny situations though, that we can all watch in those reality TV shows where people start a new life in another country and often cannot string a sentence together in the language of their new home country. I've also witnessed an English lady ask for a chicken in the Spanish local butchers, and just repeating the word in a louder and more angry tone when the butcher was looking at her as if she came from another planet; it was hilarious. And the Dutch lady who cut a piece of her farmer's cheese for the Spanish customer telling her it is "mucho lekker" (mucho delicious) and continued the conversation with Dutch words with a Spanish accent was certainly amusing. Talking about accents. I happen to have moved to Andalusia. Now those of you who come here well prepared after having attended a good few years of Spanish language classes, might still get a bit of a shock as in Andalusia they seem to speak a different language. They swallow the last letters of most words and the deeper you get into the countryside the more they seem to shorten their words. So, don't be surprised to hear 'maome' instead of 'mas o menos', which means 'more or less'. It feels as if you have to go back to school again, but don't worry, after a few years of practice you get used to the word-swallowing and might find yourself leaving out a few of the last letters of some Spanish words during a conversation with a local shopkeeper. That's when you know you are starting to blend in. Language is a funny thing. I personally love languages. This doesn't mean that I never make mistakes, in fact after almost eighteen years in Spain I still throw in the odd Italian word and I also cannot seem to master the correct use of 'take and bring' ('llevar and traer'). More importantly I still have to think carefully when I tell people that I am feeling warm, which is a much-used comment when you live here. It works perfectly well if you ask for a coffee and add 'muy caliente' to make sure that it doesn't arrive lukewarm. Especially during summertime, when many Spanish like to dump a few ice cubes in their coffee. But when I told some people that I was feeling 'muy caliente' it was received with a lot of amusement. This suggested that I was 'hot' and rather in the mood. It is also a challenge, when I write in Spanish on my mobile phone, to avoid the word 'year' as my English phone keyboard does not have the ñ. Year is 'año' but 'ano' has a very different meaning. You can look that up in a dictionary. Living in a foreign country may come with language barriers, but nothing that cannot be solved with a good laugh and a smile. Although some Spanish do make an effort to speak English this comes with a challenge for them too. Specifically, for Andalusian born Spanish, as they tend to swallow the end of their English words as well, which can make it difficult to understand them. Singing in English can be a challenge for some Spanish singers for this very reason as I found out recently during a concert. Although the voice of the singer guitarist was great. His music was fantastic as he enthusiastically sang with a strong American accent, trying to cheer up the crowds. However, his English was so bad that I could not make any sense of it and judging by the laughter of a group of English people in the audience I was not the only one. It reminded me of when I was young and sang along with the Beatles "obladi oblada la gozon yeah la la la la la gozon" years before I learned English in school. Does all this matter? I guess not. At the end of the day the most important thing is living side by side peacefully and that is exactly what I myself and many expats do. And just in case you are wondering? You are right, I am not a native English speaker, I am Dutch and my English isn't perfect but I hope you are enjoying my Spanish adventures nevertheless! "Bienvenido a España" (Welcome to Spain)

Hospital adventure

Finally, the time had come to bite the bullet and with some hesitation and feelings of fear I entered the hospital for my appointment with the surgeon to get his opinion on recurring inflammation in my legs, to be precise in my varicose veins. For some time now I had made attempts to ignore this, trying to visualise the problem away, imagining white light and tiny creatures repairing my legs. Failing miserably because, apparently, I don't trust that theory enough. In the meantime, the stress and the subconscious worry about the pain in my legs made me comfort eat, which is the opposite of what I should have been doing and I had reached a stage where my left leg looked like a Chinese vase painted by a drunken Blue Delft ceramic painter. Oh, what joy! I was worried about the doctor being super handsome while I imagined that I had to expose my middle-aged legs with possibly here and there a few tufts of hair. Not so unthinkable given the fact that my reading glasses kept falling off my nose while I bent over to shave my legs that morning. Becoming middle-aged means that the hair is creeping up. It seems to be disappearing from the lower leg area and has now reached my upper leg and groin and will soon, so I hear, move up to my face! It's a good thing that I am pretty good at pretending that I'm not in my own body, when I find myself in an embarrassing situation. This happens often enough. The door opened and there he was, Doctor Handsome. I entered the consultation room and was told that my legs were in a pretty bad shape and in desperate need of an operation. Aargh! Two weeks later, on the twelfth of April, I walked into the hospital, appropriately nervous for the operation on my left leg. After some formalities and preparation, I was taken to my hospital room for the night. The knock on the door shortly after raised my adrenaline and then having to drop my trousers in front of the surgeon and two blonde nurses in order to mark out the treatment area on my leg with a waterproof black marker felt far from comfortable. It being my first ever operation I was pretty much shocked when I was told to take off all my clothes and put on the hospital top in an uncomely baby blue with a high neckline and a seriously unflattering back. Revealing far more than I, an operation virgin, could find acceptable. An attractive youngster came to get me on a wheelchair that felt extremely unstable, leaving my vivid imagination with pictures of me rolling across the floor of the hospital hallway in utter embarrassment. But it never came to that. My ultrasound was carried out by a kind lady and I was rolled back to my room by my young companion who now told me to lie on my hospital bed. I could not help but feel rather ridiculous, as I was perfectly capable of walking to whatever destination in the hospital. I tried having a cheerful chat with my kind 'carrier' but my unusual mix of Spanish and Italian, ever so logical for a Dutch woman, was a bit too much for his understanding. I arrived at the surgery ward a little later where I was asked to lay down on another bed. My hair was held in place by what seemed like a green shower hat, making me feel increasingly less attractive, at the same time wondering why that mattered anyway! The door opened to a bright green hallway which resembled a tunnel of light. My overactive brain could easily make the comparison. I was left in a room with some other patients which, I presumed, was the recovery room, where I would await my operation. Trying to look unbothered and as if all this was very normal to me, I could not help noticing the influx of gorgeous-looking young doctors and male nurses walking in and out of the room. The scene could easily be mistaken for a Mr. Universe competition. I was painfully aware of my almost naked body beneath a thin cotton sheet and became more and more nervous. A male nurse came to check out my 'papers' and read out my name, Doña (mrs.) van 'nietje' as he pronounced it. Which in Dutch means staple, but can also be read as a 'nobody'. I clearly felt that both were appropriate given the situation. I responded with a 'more or less', referring to my name, which squeezed a smile out of his cute face. I was given a 'stent' attached to an obligatory drip of water, I was told. Probably an hour that seemed to be three hours later, the anaesthetist, yet another Mr. Handsome, and the surgeon, came in. I was suddenly surrounded, so it seemed, by an army of mouth-wateringly good-looking males whilst my bladder was trying to ignore an unstoppable urge. I had no choice, immediately prior to the operation, but to ask whether I could quickly empty my bladder first. There was no quickly about it and after a calming 'don't worry, this is normal'. The male nurse who would take me to the toilet yelled 'pipi o caca' which made my embarrassment even greater. Luckily the surgeon said. "A pipi". I was driven, on my bed, to another ward to relieve myself. Just before I was finally pushed into the operating theatre, I was introduced to two lovely young Finnish nurses who would attend my operation as part of their internship. Something I welcomed with enthusiasm, as this would help me to get some of my nervous thoughts out into the open, with a smile of course. A little later I was moved onto the operating table. The view of my bottom part was rapidly obscured from my vision by a piece of green fabric, which was just as well. I was attached to a heart monitor and a blood-pressure machine and given a medicine to calm me down. I was vaguely aware of some shaving going on down there; apparently, I missed a bit, and was soon calm and ready for whatever would come my way. Apart from my awareness of a fairly explicit position, it was not nearly as bad as I could have imagined. It was very easy to pretend that my bottom-half did not exist despite my 'exposure'. The noticeable tiny punctures and later the rather intense burning of the laser treatment and unpleasant pulling out of some side-branches of my over-sized varicose vein were at best a little awkward and painful, but by practicing meditation and going into the pain with my thoughts it became absolutely bearable. Helping me to achieve a calmness that kept my heart at a regular slow beat. Apparently, unlike most other patients who often have an increased reaction on the heart monitor at painful moments, I had unknowingly turned into an exemplary patient. Well the feeling was mutual. The atmosphere was uplifting, I chatted and told silly anecdotes – something I tend to do when feeling uncomfortable - throughout the entire operation, there was a lot of laughter going on and I was surrounded by warm and friendly experts, without doubt, and it was easy to keep a lively conversation going. Viva España! I'll be back ... To be precise on the 28th of April, for an operation on my right leg.

Women's network

I'm not sure whether it's something for me, but I'm curious. Every first Friday of the month there is a meeting with a specific theme. It sounds interesting, but I'm a little shy. Networking is important, but I am allergic to groups and to conversations about the weather, family, and topics that don't have my interest. A bit nervously I walk into the room. I am immediately pleasantly surprised by the interesting mix of the ladies present, ranging in age from mid-twenty to seventy. Artists, writers, entrepreneurs, coaches and massaging spiritual ladies of different nationalities, with or without their own healing or aroma massage practice. All independent, powerful women full of fighting spirit and ideas and plans to try and realise. Every month there is a workshop, a lecture or a demonstration. From communication and marketing to horse whispering, from a 'tapa- tasting' to fidgeting with your nipples. This month it is about so-called 'energy medicine'. My interest has been aroused because I love energy in all its forms. Apart from the fact that quantum physics fascinates me, I am attracted to people who want to grow, research, and who want me to change my mind. People, who like me, want to believe everything until the opposite is proven. A world in which the fact that something cannot be proven is not proof, a world in which everything is open and therefore possible, to the presumed annoyance of seasoned sceptics. Religions, spiritual trends and scientific research ... I find everything fascinating. But as soon as opinions become too firm and exclusion becomes part of it, I move on. The 'energy medicine' sounds interesting and I am very curious. We are welcomed by a powerful, beautiful, full-figured woman who will lead the workshop. She enthusiastically explains what energy medicine entails. It is a supplement to all possible forms of healthcare that can help to activate natural energies in the body and bring it back into balance. This is done by, among other things, massaging different energy points, also known from acupuncture, yoga and kinesiology, or by tapping on them. We learn about the energies flowing through our bodies, and that they are often blocked. We are shown how we can make our energy flow again by tapping and rubbing our body in specific points. With hilarious laughter we follow the examples that we are given and all the ladies present enthusiastically tap on their cheeks, collarbones and chest. It seems as if the energy is really going to flow. We stroke our bodies in the shape of an eight and learn that it is a good idea to regularly massage our nipples because this can prevent cancer. "If it doesn't work it doesn't hurt either", I realise and cheerfully rub my nipples just like the other networking ladies. In between the exercises I make notes in a notebook so that I cannot forget anything. After an intense hour the workshop finishes and I go home with clearly more energy than that I arrived with that morning. The many techniques, to put into practice at home, seem simple enough and I firmly believe that I will do the exercises daily. But after two days of tapping, rubbing and stroking, alone in my bedroom, my enthusiasm ebbs away. My attention is drawn back to apparently more relevant things, such as the question "How will I be able to pay the rent for next month?" I list my options: art, writing, cooking, translating ... As I create a new priority list, I feel a strong aversion to marketing and selling, but I know that it is the path I have to follow. A women's network suddenly seems like a great idea. I decide to register as an 'active member'.

57

Elves with an opinion

A few years ago, on a very hot summer's day my telephone rang. *"Hi Renate, how are you?"* asks Monica, a German lady whom I had met years earlier at an art fair. Monica asks me whether we could meet up, as her partner Gerda had 'been told' psychically that we had to exhibit our work together in a village along the coast. I was curious, so the next day I drive down the long winding mountain road to visit the remote cottage tucked away in a sea of green avocado plantations and silver-green olive trees. I turn right into a dirt track which leads to the house of Monica and Gerda and am greeted by the two large-sized ladies with big smiles on their round faces. It feels as if I am entering a delusional, fairy-tale world and I suddenly think ... "They are going to eat me!" However, I am warmly welcomed by the two 'white witches' as they call themselves. They are both wearing similar big blue dresses without sleeves with a Kangaroo-pouch pocket on the front. Their huge breasts are dangling clearly visible and freely under the thin cotton fabric. It feels soft, hot and humid during the awkwardly long hug. Messy long, grey hair is framing their white, sweaty faces, completing the picture. Makeup doesn't fit into their world. Gerda looks somewhat wild with her watery blue eyes. They tell me that she is the creative mind and the healer of the two. I am invited into their home, an oasis of calm in a wonderfully warm atmosphere. Everywhere I look I see angels, Tutankhamun replicas, ceramic sculptures and buddha images. I feel relaxed and at ease. Whilst Monica is giving me a cup of herbal tea Gerda tells me about the elves and fairies that are invisible to most people. With a mysterious smile she explains that many think she is crazy but continues very seriously that elves and fairies have told her that it is time for a joint exhibition of my art and their dresses. Monica, who attends to all Gerda's wishes, listens. There is a fairy-tale atmosphere and their strange harmonious relationship seems to work perfectly. Gerda pours me another cup of tea whilst Monica enters the living room with a large number of sweaters, jackets and dresses hand-knitted by her. I am totally amazed when I see the beautiful colours and motifs used. The cardigans and dresses have long pointed hoods that perfectly fit their pyramid-like shape. Gerda then explains that she has received a message from her elves to create square dresses. Monica leaves the room to get them and shows me a variety of thin one-size-fits-all square dresses made of thin cotton fabric. The dresses are beautifully hand-painted by Gerda with colourful symbols and flowers, birds of paradise and Egyptian motifs. They tell me to try one on and I am pleasantly surprised. For someone who never wears a dress I am filled with enthusiasm. I very much admire the work of Monica and Gerda and tell them that I feel their clothing is certainly worthy of an exhibition. They don't sell their work to the public, but Monica and Gerda have decided they would like to exhibit their dresses and cardigans alongside my paintings and ceramic sculptures. It seems like a good plan and I feel optimistic and happy when I drive back home with the exhibition date set. Two days later my phone rings ... "I am very sorry Renate", says Monica, "unfortunately the elves have told Gerda that after all it isn't the right time for an exhibition".

I can't help but feel disappointed!

'Synchrodestiny' in La Herradura

How it all began. I love the word 'synchrodestiny' which is the title of a book by Deepak Chopra. Synchronicity and destiny, how appropriate when it comes to meeting my husband. Although I had lived in La Herradura for over a year I had not seen him before, but one day, when I subconsciously was ready to move on from my life with John, I saw Miguel everywhere, whenever I walked my dog, when I went shopping or out for a coffee with a friend. It was hardly ever at the exact same time. Then he got himself a puppy Bull Mastiff and I ran into him even on a more regular basis. As if our destiny was trying to tell us something. He lived in the very same street as me, with his mother and his sisters, as I later found out. He always greeted me with a warm smile and 'hola'. With hindsight it is strange that I had not noticed him before as he had lived in the same place-all his life. Gosh, I did fancy him, but I was convinced that such an attractive man would not be single. Then some friends of mine told me they were practicing Tai Chi in the village. I had always wanted to do Tai Chi so I asked them where and when it was. As soon as I walked in, I saw him. My heart stopped, I felt silly and was afraid that he would think that I was following him, but my friends called him and introduced us. Miguel greeted me with his beautiful smile and a kiss on both cheeks, which is customary in Spain. I felt hugely uncomfortable and during the classes I could not keep my eyes off him. He was always very kind to me and I was pretty sure he liked me too, but he was also extremely shy. Weeks went by and I had never felt such a strong attraction to someone, almost to the point of heartache. One day he came out of the gate of what the Spanish call 'patio' (courtyard), just when I was walking down to go to the Tai Chi class. So, we walked down together. We started chatting and he told me that his sister also was an artist. He suggested I went to meet her, which I did a week later. She was very nice and I asked her whether she perhaps knew of a place to rent for me. The economic crisis had hit my wallet quite hard, on the one hand, because purchasing an artwork is not a priority in times of a financial crisis for most people, and also because since John had left the country it was hard for me to find a good English proof reader who could check my translations. Less work than normal came in and I was struggling to pay my five-hundred and fifty Euros per month; the rent for my apartment where I had by then lived for about eighteen months. His sister told me that her other sister had an apartment with a view to the 'patio' where Miguel lived, for three-hundred Euros a month. I told her that this would not be such a good idea (thinking he would then totally suspect I was stalking him) as his dog and mine did not get on. But she assured me that the apartment had a separate entrance in another street. I went there and I loved the place and Miguel's twin sister, who rented out the apartment was really happy with me as a new tenant, including me bringing along a cat and a dog. Miguel then offered to help me move, which I kindly accepted, but he never made a move to ask me out. I tried to be clever and organised dinner parties for his family, for friends and a goodbye party for a fellow Tai Chi member. He gladly accepted the invitation to these parties. However, he told me that he was very happy with his life and didn't want a relationship as it was better to be alone than in bad company. Two of his sisters had divorced their cheating husbands, years before that and his opinion of marriage or relationships was not good. One day I decided to invite him for lunch on his own. He accepted with a shy smile. After the meal he said he had to go. I told him "I know you don't believe in being in 'bad company', but just so you know, I think you are very good company and if you ever think that I might be good company too, you know where I live". He said we could be friends but nothing more. We started 'dating as friends with benefits' and met practically every day. A few months later he left a note on my table. "Te quiero" (I love you). Two years on we married on the beach of La Herradura and moved into our new home. We have now been together for eight years and married for six. The synchronicity that brought us together has become a stable togetherness. Our destiny has been sealed. Spain, and especially La Herradura, has now become the place where I belong.

Growing older in Spain

It is well known that a lot of pensioners choose to live or spend longer times of the year in the warm Spanish sun, and who can blame them. Everything seems to be less squeaky when you wake up with the sun warming your face. However, on the Spanish Costas there are various seaside resorts where, especially during winter months, you might wonder whether you have ended up in an open-air home for the elderly, with plenty of grey-haired silver foxes strolling along the boulevard or enjoying a coffee or a drink on one of the many pavement cafes. Their brown and sometimes weathered skin flags up as a give-away of their lifestyles but overlaid with an overdose of sunshine it all looks rather attractive. And God is kind when we get older as we start seeing each other in a lovely haze where wrinkles and age spots are non-existent, living in a bit of a blur until the glasses come out to read the menu. Those glasses that suddenly appear in our lives. So, we are living in Spain, and getting older and we all have a story to tell. Me too. I used to have excellent eyesight and I could easily read the small print on products in supermarkets, but then I started postponing the inevitable till my arms were no longer long enough to hold whatever I was trying to read. Nowadays it is a constant struggle of finding my reading glasses and swapping them for my long-distance glasses so I don't trip over a lost trolley in the middle of the aisle. The realisation that I had been using my husband's shaving cream instead of fixation foam when styling my hair every morning for quite a few weeks, thinking it was the fixation foam lying next to it in the draw of the bathroom cupboard, made me realise that my eyesight had gone down rapidly... OK, still being half asleep didn't help. On the bright side, the shaving foam worked equally well.

There is, however, another really positive side about growing older in Spain. There seems to be no age discrimination. I can only speak from my own experience in Holland where, in my hometown of Arnhem, age discrimination does happen. In the sense that the old and the young hardly mix for pleasure. In the town centre there is an area with lots of bars and pubs but every place seems to have its own age group. I remember being in my late forties, feeling like a near-death-experience - as in incredibly old - when I walked into a pub and found myself surrounded by only minus-twenty-year-olds, giving me the distinct feeling that I did not belong there. I have never felt like that in Spain and during the recent launch of my book 'Reflections from La Herradura' this became pleasantly clear to me once again. There was such a nice mix, in the La Cochera music café, of people over sixties, even over seventies, below twenty-year-olds and every age in between. Everybody is happy to accept each other, mingling in conversation, in laughter, dancing and enjoying the live music. It was a great reminder of how much I love growing old(er) in Spain. And let's be honest, considering the only alternative, the good thing about growing old is growing old.

A giant jellyfish

He finds a stick, walks into the sea and drags the huge, transparent jellyfish to the beach. It has at least a diameter of seventy-five cm and actually looks beautiful. But on a hot summer day on a popular nudist beach, jellyfish are not desirable. I look at the naked man and see how proud he is that he has managed to pull the clearly heavy marine creature out of the sea. Miguel gets up and walks over to the man to take a closer look. I realise how much more self-confidence he has than when we first entered this nudism adventure. He just walks around naked and talks to other naked Spanish people, all bent over while pricking the transparent jellyfish with sticks. She is now vulnerable on the sand and unable to slash out her tentacles to inflict a painful stab. I must admit it makes me feel sad. Surely, she has more right to be in the sea than we, humans. A crowd gathers to watch the spectacle. If there is one jellyfish it means that there are more and we quickly conclude that swimming in the beautiful cool, clear Mediterranean Sea is not a good idea today. Young boys and their fathers fish dozens of small jellyfish from the sea and triumphantly show their catch. It feels a bit wrong too, because due to overfishing, sea turtles have almost disappeared and they rely on having jellyfish as their staple diet. I watch the spectacle and Miguel comes and sits next to me. I find him so attractive. He can sometimes not hide his feelings for me and if I give him a pat, he says that he is going to think very strongly of Rajoy, at that time prime minister of Spain and certainly not attractive, to calm himself down. We laugh. The sun is hot but the cool sea breeze makes the experience very pleasant. He takes the newspaper out of the beach bag and I grab my notebook for writing, but we don't read or write. I am surprised about the different types of people on the beach, from very young to very old. All apparently totally comfortable in their body. But I do have mixed feelings and have to come to the conclusion that there are many cases of shameless exhibitionism. This mainly concerns the men. Most of the men seem to like to flaunt their dangly bits. The funny proof of this is that all men are already undressing in the parking lot and that most women only get undressed when they arrive at their place on the beach. Men like to stroll along the coast, women a lot less. What also makes me doubt the authenticity of nudism is that many of the nudists, both old and young, shave their private parts. That I'm not finding this attractive is a personal opinion, it reminds me of the innocence of young children, and young children and adult private parts don't go together in my book. But more importantly, it seems contradictory that people say they are naturalists. I've heard people say things like "nudism is pure nature, like God intended us to be, nothing to be ashamed of" but then they shave away the hair that naturally grows there. Now I have to admit that I also shaved a little this morning, but only to tidy it up and update it a bit. I always used to fall for abundantly hairy men and I could never have imagined that I would eventually fall in love with a man who once was indeed extremely hairy, but who thought it was so terrible that he decided to have the whole lot lasered away. Except for his private piece, and that is a good thing, because I would definitely have fallen out of love as quickly as I had fallen in it. Now I have more hair than he does, but he loves me nonetheless. So that's nice. There is always so much to talk and laugh about. I am surprised that I feel so relaxed, lying here in the sun, surrounded by naked people. And they watch, we all watch. It feels so completely natural and normal and yet not at all. I watch the many piercings dangling in the soft wind on the body parts of many shaved male bodies. It looks painful. This nudist beach adventure started very early in our relationship. On a Sunday morning, my love suggested going to a nudist beach to swim, practice a little nudism, and then have lunch at the beach bar. I had to think about that for a while, because normally I already feel uncomfortable on the beach in a swimsuit and I couldn't really imagine that I would dance around naked (more likely, lying on my stomach, hysterically and nervously laughing). Now living in southern Spain, I am also familiar with the term 'move south', which, as you get older, takes on a whole new meaning as certain body parts also move south. But one thing is certain. I feel very safe and OK with him. I have never felt so free and accepted in the company of a man. It is very new to me and also very good for my self-acceptance. He had never been to a nude beach, either. We decided not to put pressure on ourselves and if one of us didn't want to continue, we would just go to another beach. The first time we went he borrowed a parasol from his sister and told her he would go to the beach with me, he didn't tell her which beach. I also asked him to promise me something. I love swimming, but the idea of having to walk out of the water petrified me. On the beaches here getting out of the water means crawling out of it on hands and knees, since it is a pebbled beach. It is definitely a challenge to walk out of the sea like an Ursula Andress Bond girl. So, he promised to come and get me every time I wanted to get out of the water to walk back to my towel. We were both very nervous but decided to go for it. We had never done anything like that and it made it very special. On the beach we found a spot near the sea. We whipped off our clothes and lay down. Giggling like a pair of teenagers. We had also set up a parasol and he said "I hope the parasol doesn't fly away." We laughed while we imagined that he had to run after the parasol. Which then of course happened. It was so funny, the 'law of attraction' in full operation! That summer we went back to the beach several times. It was liberating, but it also had something very nasty. There were far too many exhibitionists on the beach to my taste, who ruined it for the 'real naturalists' if you can call them that. There was also a large row of bamboo plants on the edge of the beach, behind which open spaces were hidden from view by the bamboo. It was a coming and going of homosexual men who met there and came back with a rosy smile on their faces. I have nothing against that but feel no need to witness it. When we went to the beach at the end of the season and I realised that there were mainly men on the beach and I saw an older guy who was openly playing with his bits I told Miguel that I wanted to go home and never return. He lovingly agreed and we never went back.

A smoky adventure

I was shaking whilst sitting on a cold iron bench at the bus stop, waiting for my bus to my ceramic class. It wasn't an earthquake but an elegantly dressed Spanish lady. Her leg was nervously making rapid movements which made the bench vibrate. My fantasy took her along on a journey of possibilities. From a dentist visit to an appointment with her lover to tell him that she was going to leave him. I was soon distracted from my thoughts by the spring bird song in the tall trees on the small roundabout in front of the bus stop. It was January and rather worrying to hear these migrating birds singing their beautiful song. A far too mild winter, with far too little rain is confusing the local flora and fauna. I didn't get much time to think about that as the bus arrived and I had to prepare myself for my weekly discussion with the bus driver. I have to get off at a bus stop that is not very familiar to most drivers and for some reason I have seen a different bus driver every week, which means I have to explain, plead and put my foot down to be allowed on the bus. This day was no exception. When I mentioned my destination the initial reaction from the bus driver, like most weeks, was "I don't stop there". I then insisted and explained where it was and mentioned some landmarks. This usually does the trick, but this time it didn't. The bus driver wasn't having it and told me there was no such bus stop. The queue behind me was growing but I remained calm and friendly telling him that I was taken there every week and that he could check the existence of the bus stop on his digital ticket machine. Reluctantly he did and I was allowed on the bus. I sat down on one of the faded chairs and looked at the chair in front of me which said "fasten seat belt" a reminder of the long-distance international trips of these now local buses. The seat belts had been taken out and nobody, apart from me, seemed to think that this half an hour journey, for some even longer, along a bendy road, often next to sheer drops down to the sea, with, it has to be said, breath-taking views, is a good enough reason to fasten a seat belt. I said a little prayer and sent some white light to the grumpy driver to get me safely to my destination. It worked, and I walked into the ceramic studio all in one piece. It was a special day and I was nervous. I have done ceramics for many years but I had not experimented much with glazing and I also had never done Raku. This was my main reason to join the ceramics class with a nice mixed group of people, (English and Spanish, me being the only Dutch person) both beginners and professional artists. It was my very first Raku firing experience and I came prepared with a mask as I was told it would be a smoky event. Our teacher was an interesting, very knowledgeable, sweet bodybuilder, usually scarcely dressed in shorts and a vest, both summer and winter. Most nights he was 'delighting' us with the smell of his four boiled egg whites that he brought along in a Tupperware box and consumed during the ceramic class. For the occasion he wore some highly flammable sports trousers, which I found rather worrying. He had been firing up a kiln earlier that day, filled with my statues that had been painted with special Raku glaze. After the class, when most of my classmates had left, the kiln was opened. It was an amazing spectacle. The red-hot statues were taken out with a special tool and then dropped into an old oil barrel filled with sawdust. Every time the teacher had dropped a ceramic object into the barrel, we rapidly added a few handfuls of sawdust, which of course caught fire immediately. As soon as all the statues were in the barrel it was topped up with even more of the stuff. Then the lid was quickly put on the barrel and subsequently covered with a wet cloth. There was smoke, a lot of smoke, so we made sure to wait at a safe distance. Approximately fifteen minutes later the statues were taken out of the barrel and put into a big basin filled with cold water, to then be cleaned with a hard brush under a running tap, revealing the end result. The colours were stunning, a mixture of purple, blue and copper with silver and turquoise touches. Reminding me of the colours of an oil leak on a puddle of water, which is of course only stunning colour wise. My statues turned out better than I could have hoped for, it was a magic moment. My hair, my skin and clothes were smelling like a wood log burned in an open fire, but I didn't care. With my statues safely wrapped up for the journey back, I returned home. It had been a great and satisfying adventure. Three days later I was lying in bed and shaking. There was no Spanish lady to be seen. It was an earthquake, 6.5 on the Richter scale, which had woken up the entire Malaga and Granada coast region!

Christmas with a difference

My Dutch family wasn't very traditional and I cannot even remember having spent many Christmases together. Christmas has only grown into a commercial celebration in Holland over the last decades or so. When I was a child, it was merely a period of spending time with family and friends and having some Christmas decorations in the house. Giving gifts was not part of it. As a young adult I used to spend either Christmas day or Boxing Day at my parent's house for a meal and to just be together. But if I didn't feel like it, it wasn't a big deal. It certainly wasn't an obligation. There also was no typical Christmas food tradition in The Netherlands, apart from some seasonal sweets. It was more about extravagance in foods that we did not eat during the year and of course, the obligatory too much of whatever was served. On New Year's Eve my brother and I were usually dragged off to some party, with lots of traditional 'oliebollen' which literally translates into 'oil balls'. Don't be fooled though, as they are delicious balls of dough, deep-fried and covered with powdered sugar. I suppose they could best be described as a doughnut type snack, but lighter and fluffier. Midnight was always amazing with the typical Dutch custom of firework displays by most families in every street and neighbourhood, turning the entire country, for at least fifteen minutes or so, into a colourful display of lights and explosions. People going out into the streets with a glass of bubbles to start the New year, wishing everybody the best! Then I met an English man and together we moved to Spain. Christmas became a tradition and soon I found my myself sitting in front of the television watching English shows with a silly paper hat on and a Christmas cracker in my hand. A fake nylon Christmas tree with cheap shiny balls, tinsels and lights were taken out of the box each year to be set up in some corner and then, during the weeks leading up to Christmas, lots of small gifts wrapped in shiny paper were accumulating below the tree. I loved it. My now ex-partner being an excellent cook also insisted in preparing a typical English Xmas meal every year, including all the veggies and Yorkshire pudding. The left-overs turned into a fantastic bubble and squeak that we ate on Boxing Day. Christmas decorations in Spain weren't as over the top as we had known them to be in Holland and the UK, but the Christmas tree in the square and light decorations over the streets certainly brought us into a festive spirit. Then I married a Spanish man and got an entire family with it. The outside Christmas decorations were still the same and in some cities like Malaga they have turned it into a true art with lots of lights, certainly worth a visit. Another sure sign that the festive season had arrived is a television in a corner of the local bar or restaurant with children singing the winning numbers of the Christmas lottery to some boring tunes, and groups of people from a local choir going around the village singing songs to collect money for charity, the Spanish equivalent of carol singers. However, to me personally this festive season got a whole new meaning when I got to know the family traditions. Now at best I fail to understand why many of the Spanish people living in southern Spain don't do heating and my 'new' family is no exception. Their excuse that it doesn't really get cold and winter lasts only a couple of months is not very true as many expats living here can confirm. Oh yes, winters can be like northern European summers with temperatures over twenty degrees during the day, but when the sun goes down the temperature drops below ten degrees, not only outside but also indoors. Many houses are built to keep the sun out and no natural heat is coming in. So, out come the jumpers, many layers of them, and the highly inflammable, nylon dressing gowns that are put on as a final layer. There sometimes is a round table with a small under-table heater to provide some warmth to a cold body. Cold and cracked dry skin on the hands and a runny nose don't seem to bother them. Now that my circumstances have changed and I am married I have found out that my Spanish family is no different. My mother-in-law, a tiny, possibly due to old-age shrinkage, feisty and very funny lady (who sadly died in January of 2019 at the age of 85) could barely walk as she shuffled out onto the patio in her four or five layers of jumpers and trousers, to sit in the sun to heat up her frozen legs. The under-table heating was only used by her as an exception as she was used to a lifetime of saving up for the kids and spending the least possible on herself. She would not have had it any other way. The December holiday makes no exception, heating still doesn't exist. It took some time for me to get used to Christmas with my new family. Spain doesn't acknowledge a second Christmas day or a Boxing Day so the festivities are squeezed into Christmas Eve, where the family enjoys a meal together and Christmas day where the family enjoys lunch together. The lucky ones get to sit at the table with the under-table heating, some holding the table-cloth underneath their chins to get maximum effect of the welcoming heat. Houses can get very cold in southern Spain as many are built to keep the sun out. If you don't get to sit at the table with the heating underneath you have no option but to come in layers or to keep your coat on. No Christmas tree or decoration to create a festive atmosphere and gifts are only given to the two young children in the family on Christmas Eve. Another tradition is to eat fish soup and lots of prawns, big prawns usually, which come with some side dishes and too many deserts and seasonal fried cookies and other sweet treats. The leftovers are then eaten on Christmas Day. I'm not a great fan of prawns, especially not loads of them and I really don't like fish soup. Christmas has become my least favourite part of the year. Luckily there is no obligation to spend the entire Xmas Eve or day together so when the last bite of super sweet dessert has been eagerly digested, everybody rushes out to do whatever they fancy doing that day. After having taken part in two of such Christmases I suggested to Miguel that we could break that family tradition as we are living in our welcoming house with a wonderful wood pellet-stove, which was a serious condition for me even considering getting married. The pellet-stove nicely heats up the entire house and creates a wonderful atmosphere with its real flames. We suggested celebrating Christmas Eve at our place, and that has now become a new family tradition. A fake Christmas tree in the corner of the room with sparkly Christmas lights, a pleasant heat, no more coats on or runny noses, just a lot of cooking for me, but fortunately that is one of my hobbies. So far, they've enjoyed (I hope) an international tapas meal (twelve different tapas), a Chinese meal, a typical Dutch meal with traditional Dutch food, a Tai and Indian meal and a vegan meal. I'm now running out of ideas, but the vegan tradition will be continued as Miguel and I are now on an eighty-ninety percent vegan diet and feeling loads better on this. The visitors bring the desserts. And New Year's Eve? According to another family tradition that is spent in the house of one of my sisters-in-law. A very cold house. She has a huge open fireplace, but never bothers to light it. We sit there with thick jumpers or our coats on, a television is showing silly sketches by men dressed up as women, slightly too loud. The family cheerfully recalls some curious past events in the local village. The meal consists mainly of meat dishes, something that has never been to my taste, so I usually indulge in bread with 'aioli'. After having seen too many cute piglets, cuddly cows and happily jumping-about lambs with colourful knitted jumpers, all saved from the slaughterhouse, on Facebook I can no longer eat meat, even if it is disguised as a tasty pate or sliced salami. Guess I'll be bringing my own dinner next time. At midnight we all pop twelve grapes into our mouths on the counts of the last twelve seconds of the passing year. A few hugs and kisses and best wishes and off we go... usually home to sleep off the exhaustion of the stressful Christmas season and with the full intention to comply with our New Year's resolution to never host another meal again! But, as is the case with so many well-intended resolutions, I'm already thinking of new, original, vegan recipes for yet another Christmas Eve.

Avocados, an adventure in taste and love

The first few times I went to the avocado 'cortijo' (farm) with my Miguel, I wasn't really interested in the avocados as we could not keep our hands off each other. But as these things go, lust turns into love and a whole new world opened up to me. A world of avocados. Little did I know. I suddenly received fresh avocados by the dozen, and at first I really didn't know what to do with them, apart from using them to create a Mexican style guacamole and making friends happy, as I could not possibly eat them all. I was fascinated by what running an avocado farm actually entails and how many varieties there are. Miguel took over the three hectares 'cortijo' in 1983, when he was only eighteen years old, but he still continued to go to college. His uncle helped him and taught him all the fine tricks of looking after this wonderful crop. When Miguel took over the farm it was mostly an almond tree farm with some 'nisperos' (loquats) and 'cherimoya' (custard apple) trees. However, he chopped down all the almond trees but one, and planted the 'bacon' avocado variety. At the time it was the best known avocado in Spain. I didn't know avocados weren't native to Spain, but they actually originate from countries like Mexico and Guatemala and there are more than fifty different types. Even more surprising to me was that they are botanically classified as a berry. Miguel loves talking about avocados and to explain to people that he only grows five varieties. The most known avocados are Bacon, the first one picked as early as September-October, and Hass and Fuerte. These last two are the ones you are most likely to find in supermarkets all over the world. The 'cortijo' is an enchanting place and the very first time that I went there with Miguel I fell in love with him even more after I saw him kissing the leaves of one of his avocado trees. He was so proud. The trees made him calm and happy, that was very obvious. There is also a small building on the 'cortijo' where he enjoys his breakfast and where we regularly go to have a meal with friends or visiting family from the Netherlands. It used to be a shed that Miguel and his family turned into a small dwelling with a bathroom with bright orange and yellow furniture, a tiny kitchen with a two-pit, top-stove fuelled by a gas bottle, and a small living space with a two-seater and a coffee table. There is no separate bedroom, but there is a bed as well. No one ever sleeps there as in the winter it is too cold and humid and in the summer you'll be eaten alive by mosquitos. Outside the building is a fairly large terrace with a table and chairs and a wood-fired bread oven. When his mother was still alive Miguel and his mother and sisters went to the 'cortijo' regularly to make lots of bread loaves for the entire family. Although I love the idea, I have too many other things that I want to do and this type of time-consuming bread baking is not one of them. When we invite people to the 'cortijo' they always like to be shown around and soak up the information, told by an enthusiastic Miguel and translated by me. People don't realise how much work goes into creating these wonderful 'berries' and how much it costs to produce them. Apart from the huge electricity expenses to keep the water pumps working, the amount of water needed is mind blowing. There are about 450 avocado trees on the farm, which is considered small-scale farming. During the summer months, and there seem to be increasingly more due to climate change, especially in July and August, each tree needs 96 litres of water a day. And water is very expensive here, more expensive, so I've been told than in The Netherlands, for example. But I guess that's to be expected when you live on the Costa Tropical as the area where we live is called. I was also really happy to find out that we were able to have fresh avocados all year round as they can stay on the tree for an entire year. Not every variety is suitable for that, as the Bacon, for example, has a thin skin and would be eaten by rats if left on the trees for too long. Miguel takes his fruit to a cooperative, but always keeps one tree for the family. He usually saves a Hass tree as it has a thicker skin. The avocados just get richer and richer in fat content and are utterly delicious. In case you are wondering, they do not ripen on the tree. All avocados are picked when hard and ripen, like bananas, off the tree. Miguel loves his job and his trees and it is beautiful to see that. Of course, it comes with worries. Will there be enough water? When it doesn't rain enough salty water from the sea can mix in with the natural water reservoirs which is disastrous for the avocado trees as well as for other plants. Will the trees get affected by a fungus? Will people who are hiking in the hills pick the avocados, stealing in fact, although they don't even consider that it is stealing? Many don't seem to realise there is a huge investment for the farmer and it's something I try to make people aware of. This investment is obviously also reflected in the price in the shops. We sometimes give guided tours in the 'cortijo' with a tapas lunch that I prepare, as I love cooking. I always make sure that I include a number of avocado tapas. Our life, to some extent, revolves around the avocados. We cannot go on a holiday as Miguel cannot leave the farm. During late spring and summer Miguel has to go there every day to sort out the water, check whether the wild boars haven't pinched one of the water supplies and get rid of weeds, which he does with a hand-held machine.

As of 2022 the farm will be officially organic. In reality it has been for some time, but it takes a few years to get all the paperwork done. I'm delighted by that as we always eat organic and it is something I'm really passionate about. The picking season starts late September in Spain starting with the Bacon. Each variety is picked in a different month and the last avocados to be picked are of the Reed variety, at the end of March or early April. After the summer international clients are demanding avocados, which results in many farmers picking the fruit too early. They get more money this way, but when you buy your fruit in the supermarket and it looks ripe on the outside and is hard and pretty tasteless on the inside you can be pretty sure it has been picked too early. Miguel works with one of the biggest cooperatives here in southern Spain and they don't start picking until the fruits are sufficiently ripe. This way the avocados shipped both abroad and throughout Spain will be perfect when you purchase them from your local shop or supermarket. And when you do, make sure to try out the following recipes!

Orange avocado

A delicious, typical tapa (can also be eaten as a salad) from Andalusia.

You need: 1 big orange, a juicy, sweet one preferable, like a navel orange.

1 avocado. Cut both the orange and the avocado in chunks, then sprinkle with some salt. I use herbal salt, and then a good splash of extra virgin olive oil. Eat with some fresh bread. Very delicious!

No time to cook avocado

Honestly, my favourite way of eating avocados is simply mashed and directly on a freshly toasted piece of bread and a sprinkle of herbal salt. But, also not to be sniffed at is when you add a crushed clove of garlic. If you prepare this in advance make sure you add some lemon juice to avoid the avocado from turning brown.

Fishy avocados

I'm 90% whole-food plant based, but that's another book. We don't eat meat, but during weekends we occasionally eat some fish, eggs and even some cheese. So, I will share our favourite 'fishy' avocado recipes.

Recipe one: Mash an avocado, add a little bit of lemon juice, just a sprinkle to not make it go brown. Divide on slices of toasted rustic bread and then put a salty anchovy's fillet on top of it.

Recipe two: Half an avocado, scoop out the flesh and throw away the seed (although you can use the seed as well. Google will provide you with plenty of tips for that). Make sure you don't break the skin as you will fill it again. Mash and then mix the avocado with a fork with some tuna fish from a tin, some lemon juice, a small piece of raw onion, finally chopped and a scoop of mayonnaise. Sorry you have to work out the measurements by taste. You can, if you like add a sprinkle of salt and then scoop it back into your avocado. If it survives the trip to the fridge and before serving you can add a bit of fresh parsley on the top, but no real need!

Toms and Avos

I like a simple avocado and tomato salad. All you need is an avocado, some tasty tomatoes and some finely chopped garlic. Chop the avocado and tomatoes in chunks, add the garlic and a sprinkle of salt to taste and then a good splash of extra virgin olive oil. We like to eat this with rustic bread.

To make it a bit different, but also nice, in my opinion ... add a splash of balsamic vinegar and some agave syrup. For an even fancier salad, you can add some thinly sliced red onion and some capers to taste.

What's life without a dessert?

This is a "lime-key pie in a glass" suggestion. Depending on how many people you want to feed or how hungry you are, you can adjust measurements. Take 4 ripe avocados. Scoop them out. Mix in 120-gram agave syrup, the juice of 4 limes, the zest of 2 limes and a pinch of salt. Now you can also use lemon, but then adjust a little as you don't want it too sharp. You can also add 170-gram of coconut oil. Then it will really stiffen up when you put it in a fridge, but I normally use 2 or 3 tablespoons of chia seeds instead (which gives it a nice crunch and considerably reduces the calories).

You can use 300 grams of nuts (of your choice, or a mix of nuts), 100-gram of pitted dates for the base in the glasses. Just add the date and nut mixture into a food processor till you have a gluey substance with still some crunchy bits of nuts in there. Divide the mixture over 4 or 6 glasses (again, it depends on how many desserts you want to make) and top with the avocado mixture. Put in the fridge until you eat it.

Buon appetit!

A wedding and a funeral

I haven't been to many weddings in my life, so it's fair to say that I don't have much of a clue regarding weddings. I often hear women say that every girl dreams about a beautiful wedding, but I can honestly say that I've never had that dream. The idea of having to wear an uber expensive glittery, shiny dress was more like a nightmare to me. But then I moved to Spain and met my now husband, Miguel. So, I was reborn or you could say 'life begins at fifty-five' as that was my age when Miguel and I got married on a sunny day in June. We kept it simple and had a wonderful ceremony on the beach with a small group of friends and family. And said the 'yes-word' in a heart made of pebbles. Our wedding rings were eighteen Euros each and my wedding frog ten Euros. Miguel still had a nice set of trousers and a jacket from a year prior to our wedding when we had been invited to a wedding in The Netherlands. After the ceremony we went to the patio. I had prepared a lot of different plates of food together with my cousin, a friend and Miguel's sister. Another friend had brought his guitar and my husband's cousin serenaded me in typical flamenco singing style whilst my mother-in-law was playing the castanets. It was the perfect wedding and it felt like being in a film. We did not go on a honeymoon, as the renovation costs of the house were quite high and Miguel, an avocado farmer, also cannot and does not want to leave his land unattended for more than a day. But we live in a place where people go for their holidays so I did not have a problem with that. Our life together could begin. A few weeks into our marriage I got totally depressed. I suddenly realised that I had married a Spanish family. In particular one of his sisters, who is in itself a very kind woman, did not really consider my privacy. The difference in culture did become apparent. She came to our house every day with food for my husband, telling me that he loved her food. It very much irritated me as I love cooking and wanted to cook for him. I did not want to tell her off, but it made me feel unwelcome. Before we got together Miguel had always lived with his mother and both his mother and his oldest sister prepared his food. His sister was so used to 'feeding' him that it was hard for her to let that go. So, what happened was sort of understandable. I didn't want to hurt her feelings, so I politely accepted, but it did give me a sense of not being heard, as I had told her several times that she didn't have to do that. My sister-in-law also liked our renovated house so much that, almost on a daily basis, she came at any God-given hour to show our house to whomever wanted to see it. Even those who didn't want to see it, as became clear to me from the uncomfortable look on the faces of some colleagues who were dragged to our home at eleven o'clock at night. Our house was the house where the entire family had grown up and in some strange kind of way, she seemed to feel that it is still her house too. It is part of the family. Having left my parents' house at eighteen and having travelled the world on my own, this certainly came as a shock to me. I was happy to discover that after a few months the stream of friends and colleagues dried up and we could resume our married life. But it had totally affected my sense of privacy. I realised that I was married to a Spanish family. In addition to my husband's family the patio houses three dogs and four cats, which is absolutely fine by me as I love animals, but living with a Spanish family is a challenge as they have a different idea about privacy where family is concerned. Our house has large windows with a view to a spectacular patio, full with lush plants and many flowers. It is a shared patio with his two sisters and husbands and a niece with kids. As a Dutch woman I was used to having large windows to let lots of light come in and not being bothered by people peeking in. However, because of the events in the beginning of our marriage, I started feeling like I was living in a fishbowl, I felt observed and uncomfortable and I got into the habit of keeping our thin curtains shut. It was also not so easy for my mother-in-law to have to let go of her son after forty-eight years of living with him. After her husband died, when Miguel was only twelve years old, he had to become the man of the house. Before we got married, during moments when I was alone with his mother, she often told me subtly that she didn't want another man as she already had one. She referred to Miguel. I understood her feelings, but it wasn't always easy. However, after we got married, she accepted me and told me "I'm glad you have married my son, because I don't like the idea of him being alone after I die". Three years later she fell ill with Alzheimer. A two-year period of deterioration followed. It was extremely hard for my husband and his sisters as they took turns to take care of her, day and night. The last half year she did not recognise anybody anymore and was living in the past. However, she confused my husband with her husband, who had died so many years ago. She told him, almost on a daily basis, that he had to go to the priest to sort out their wedding. Often, she accused him of having left her for 'another woman'. I was the other woman. In January of 2019 she died peacefully in her sleep. Although there was a lot of sadness for the children, as their mother had died, there was also immediate relief. Surely, if she would have had a say in it, she too would have been happy to be reunited with her husband on the other side. The fact that I live in a different culture became once again very apparent to me. She was taken to the house of another daughter only a few hours after she had died, by the funeral people. A large room was prepared with chairs against the wall for the wake. In the Netherlands, the funeral takes place within six working days, but no sooner than thirty-six hours after the person has passed away. Not sure why. Perhaps to give someone a chance to get back to life? But in Spain it usually takes place the next day. The coffin of my mother-in-law was placed in the middle of the room. In the Netherlands people are informed about and invited to a funeral via the post. But in Spain, in the small village where I live, this goes by word of mouth. People are told about the fact that someone has died by the church bells that ring in a specific way. So, they ask each other who died and there is always someone who knows. As the wife of the son I was present at the wake. My husband and I were also asked to go to the cemetery to point out the grave of the father, as the mother would be joined with him in that same grave. The Town Hall workman, in dirty clothes, asked us whether we wanted the father to be joined in the coffin with the mother or next to the coffin. My husband and sisters had decided on next to the coffin. It was freezing cold in the house. Everybody was sitting there with their coats on. No drinks or snacks were offered and the entire day people were coming and going, usually staying for at least half an hour to a couple of hours, chatting about who else was nearly dead or had just died. I was kissed by what felt like the entire village. People who I did not know, some I knew by face and never greeted me, and those who I did know. I felt out of place but was there for the support of my Miguel. We did leave for lunch and later for dinner. I went home for the night to stay with our dogs, but Miguel and his sisters stayed throughout the night. The following morning, we all went to the mass for his mother. The coffin was carried by my husband and a few other family members and when I asked whether I could do something I was given one of the flower garlands and had to walk in front of the coffin. I had never been in a similar situation and had no idea what would happen next. The mass was a typical Catholic mass and afterwards we, and just a few close family members, went to the cemetery. The workman helped put the coffin in the space in the wall. He had already put the remains of the father in a large white plastic bag, which was casually placed on the floor. It almost didn't fit next to the coffin of the mother and he had to push with all his force. To me it felt like being in a weird film, with total disrespect for the family and the deceased person. However, nobody else seemed to feel that way. We all went home after that. No coffee and cake after the funeral, as is the custom in The Netherlands. A week later there was another mass for people who had not been able to come to the first one and that was it. The mother is no longer with us, 'bless her', but she still haunts the house in the patio where she has lived with my husband for such a long time. My father found this out when he last visited me and stayed in the house, waking up at night from footsteps downstairs. Throughout the years I have learned to accept the cultural differences. A wedding and a funeral later, my Spanish family is in my life to stay.

New adventures and challenges come my way, but that is part of life. One thing is certain. Even though I love Italy, Spain, and especially La Herradura, is now my home.

About the author

Internationally exhibited artist turned published writer, Dutch born Renate van Nijen settled in Andalucía, Spain in 2004, where she continues to paint, teach art classes, and embraces her passion for writing. Before coming to Spain Renate lived in various countries. Having lived in different cultures has turned her into a compassionate, open minded artist and writer. Her art ranges from colourful women and spirit animals to Buddha impressions, flamenco dancers and mandalas. Her books cover many different subjects. From 'Cheers' about alcoholism and its effects on those close to the alcoholic, to her book 'Secret Thoughts', a collection of very short sensual, quirky stories; She also wrote 'Reflections from La Herradura' an anthology of artists of all fields in the village of La Herradura, and 'Memories of World War II' an intriguing account of her father's experience as a teenager in occupied Holland during the Second World War, She continues to write her books with humour, passion and love for the 'human-kind'! Renate's art and books are all communicating her message. Her paintings tell a story and her books paint a picture of situations that others can recognise.

To find out more about Renate's books and art feel free to visit her website: www.renatevannijen.com

Cover Artwork by Renate van Nijen

Renate has published various books and she uses one of her own paintings for the cover of each book.

The painting used for Tapas of Tales is called Rosetta and refers to the rosette of a flamenco guitar. It was painted during an international symposium where the artists created several paintings during a week of live painting.

*****